AMERICAN NEUTRALITY AND THE
SPANISH CIVIL WAR

Problems in American Civilization

UNDER THE EDITORIAL DIRECTION OF *George Rogers Taylor*

AMERICAN NEUTRALITY AND THE SPANISH CIVIL WAR

EDITED WITH AN INTRODUCTION BY

Allen Guttmann

AMHERST COLLEGE

Problems in American Civilization

D. C. HEATH AND COMPANY: Boston

INTRODUCTION

ALTHOUGH Franklin Roosevelt realized that the American economy is tied inextricably to the economies of other nations, he thought of the New Deal as a primarily domestic program. He hoped to unknot American problems without "entanglement" abroad. Like other presidents who have shared his hopes, he was disappointed. Adolf Hitler came to power the same year that Roosevelt did. On March 7, 1936, Hitler reoccupied the Rhineland and began his long campaign for *Lebensraum*. In Benito Mussolini, whose Fascist troops had invaded Ethiopia in 1935, Hitler found a ready ally.

Then came the Spanish Civil War. The Spanish Republic of 1931 was attacked by its own generals on July 17, 1936. Spain was ideologically fragmented into contentious factions—Fascists, Monarchists, Liberals, Communists, Socialists, Anarchists. Americans of every commitment found Spaniards with whom to identify. Americans *did* identify. They took sides. Some wrote passionate letters or articles; some raised money or led protest rallies; some journeyed to Spain and fought in the International Brigades. The intervention, on opposite sides, of Germany and Italy and the Soviet Union intensified the feelings of Americans who watched the Spanish Civil War as a kind of limited Armageddon. For a whole generation, Spain became the focus of hope and fear.

Under British prodding, the French Government of Léon Blum proposed a Non-Intervention Committee. The Committee, which met for the first time on September 9, 1936, consisted of twenty-seven nations pledged not to intervene in the Spanish conflict. President Roosevelt had already taken steps to achieve American neutrality. On August 7, 1936, Acting Secretary of State William Phillips notified American officials in Spain that the United States would "scrupulously refrain from any interference whatsoever in the unfortunate Spanish situation." One week later, at Chautauqua, New York, President Roosevelt laid down the policy of the "moral embargo." Since the American Neutrality Act of 1935—passed in response to Mussolini's invasion of Ethiopia—did not cover civil wars, the President asked patriotic Americans not to sell or transport munitions to Spain. He denounced the "thousands of Americans" who sought "immediate riches" even at the risk of involving their nation in war. But Robert Cuse, an American businessman, refused to accept the "moral embargo." He asked licenses to export $2,777,000 worth of aircraft materials to Republican Spain on the *Mar Cantábrico*. As the ship loaded in New York harbor, the President requested emergency legislation that effectively halted almost all American trade with Spain. (The Texaco corporation successfully supplied General Franco with oil, but this success was exceptional.) The embargo remained in effect throughout the duration of the war.

American opinion was badly divided on the wisdom of this embargo, and still is. The materials which follow provide the elementary historical facts of the Spanish Civil War, the documents which embody the embargo controversy from its origins through bitterest controversy to the end of the war, and two judgments which have the advantage of a quarter century's hindsight. The documents, which are described more fully in the headnotes, include editorials, congressional debates, open letters, magazine articles, and telegrams. The two articles which conclude the readings are based on two lectures given at Amherst College. As their sharp disagreement suggests, the issues posed by the embargo of January 8, 1937, are still unsolved. Moreover, Falangist Spain still troubles many whose stand against Communism is taken in the name of freedom. And, as the controversy over the alleged Communism of Fidel Castro's Cuba seems more and more to resemble the arguments over the Spanish Republic, the relevance of our past difficulties for an understanding of our present ones becomes ever more clear.

The specific questions raised by the Spanish Civil War are difficult enough. Should the President have departed so from American traditions? *Did* he really depart from them? Should the President have been responsive to Protestant opinion rather than to Catholic opinion, to Leftists rather than to Rightists? Should he have done *more* to insure American neutrality? Should he have exercised the powers of his office to lead Americans away from isolationism? Beyond these specific questions are still more puzzling general considerations. What is the role of religious bodies in the formation of public opinion? What is the role of public opinion in the formation of foreign policy? What is the President's responsibility in foreign affairs? Congress's? Moving to a more general level yet, we can ask other questions: Can the United States remain neutral while war rages *anywhere* on earth? Is our power such that anything we do is a form of intervention? Finally, to move from political queries to moral ones, can a peaceful world be won by force? Can one pursue a moral goal by immoral means, with the help of immoral allies? Can the ideals of Jesus of Nazareth be enforced by bombers, missiles, and—in the latest jargon—Doomsday Machines?

CONTENTS

THE CLASH OF ISSUES

Congressmen are quick to support the President's request for an arms embargo:

We have to determine our neutrality policy. We have to determine now whether we will sacrifice war profits and blood money in order to keep out of . . . wars. . . . You can almost hear the beating of the wings of the Angel of Death as it hovers over Spain tonight. . . . We peace-loving Americans have to determine whether we will sacrifice the war profits that dragged us into the last war by adopting a strict, permanent neutrality policy prohibiting the sale and shipment of arms and munitions of war to . . . belligerent countries.

HAMILTON FISH, JR.

Specialists in international law are worried by the laws passed:

This [Neutrality Act of 1937] was thought to be neutrality legislation. But it seems more like the precise opposite.

EDWIN BORCHARD

Americans opposed to the embargo agitate for its repeal:

It is on record that the chief influence [on behalf of] the iniquitous Spanish embargo has been President Roosevelt. . . . We condemn this conduct . . . as opposed to our best interests.

NEW YORK STATE SOCIALIST PARTY

Other Americans charge that anti-embargo fervor is part of a Communist conspiracy:

The frontic [sic] efforts of the Left-wingers to stir up trouble, to incite hatred, to embroil the United States is merely another illustration of the desperate character of their predicament. . . . The motto of clear-sighted, democratic, liberty-loving citizens everywhere is crystallized in these words: KEEP THE EMBARGO ON ARMS; KEEP THIS COUNTRY OUT OF WAR!

JOSEPH F. THORNING

Looking back, one American official has regrets:

Of all our blind isolationist policies, the most disastrous was our attitude on the Spanish Civil War.

SUMNER WELLES

But a prominent historian defends American policy in a larger context:

The central significance of the Spanish Civil War was its rescue of Spain from the fate which later befell the nations of eastern Europe. . . . The Spanish struggle was a prelude not so much to the Second World War as to the subsequent "cold war" and the struggle in Korea.

CARLTON J. H. HAYES

I. HISTORICAL BACKGROUND

A. L. Burt: AMERICAN FOREIGN POLICY IN THE 1930's

In 1943, Allan Nevins and Louis M. Hacker, two Columbia University historians of international reputation, edited a series of articles entitled The United States and Its Place in World Affairs. *The book was a scholarly effort to state as objectively as possible (but not without interpretations) the diplomatic history of the United States from the end of World War I. Alfred L. Burt, Professor of History at the University of Minnesota, contributed the chapters here reprinted, chapters which supply the details necessary for an understanding of American foreign policy during the 1930's.*

THE depression dominated the foreign relations of the United States during the early years of the New Deal. The foreign policy with which the new administration began resembled that with which the old administration ended. It was international cooperation in economic as well as political affairs. But Mr. Hoover's policy was to restore the conditions of the twenties when international trade was supported by lending, whereas Mr. Roosevelt's policy promised a restoration of international trade by a reduction of the artificial barriers that had been raised between nations.

The Democratic platform roundly condemned "the Hawley-Smoot tariff law, the prohibitive rates of which have resulted in retaliatory action by more than forty countries, created international economic hostilities, destroyed international trade, driven our factories into foreign countries, robbed the American farmer of his foreign markets and increased his cost of production." It called for "reciprocal tariff agreements with other nations and an international economic conference designed to restore international trade and facilitate exchange." During the election campaign, the successful Presidential candidate repeatedly developed this theme, laying upon the Republican administration much of the blame for bringing on the depression and increasing its severity by driving the world into a suicidal economic nationalism, and insisting that there could be no substantial progress toward recovery without reversing the process through international collaboration.

THE WORLD ECONOMIC CONFERENCE

The calling of an international economic conference was not a one-party proposal. The Hoover administration adopted it too, as the result of a European suggestion made about the very time that the Democrats put it in their platform. It was embodied in the final act of the Lausanne Conference, which advised the League of Nations to call such a conference and to invite the United States to participate in it. The American government then accepted the invitation

From A. L. Burt, *American Foreign Policy in the 1930's.* Reprinted from Allan Nevins and Louis M. Hacker, eds., *The United States and Its Place in World Affairs* (Boston: D. C. Heath and Company, 1943), pp. 375–409.

on the condition that all consideration of reparations, war debts, and tariff rates be excluded. As these three problems were largely responsible for the economic dislocation of the world, such a condition would cripple the conference. But it was obviously impossible for the conference to accomplish anything without American cooperation, and so it was called under the severe limitations imposed by the United States.

A commission of experts got to work in Geneva on plans for the conference; and shortly after the new administration took office in Washington, representatives from the more important countries except Russia, which had not yet entered the League nor been recognized by the United States, were invited to the United States for informal discussions. In these discussions, the date was set for the opening of the conference, and a tariff truce was arranged to last until the gathering closed. Then in a broadcast to the world on May 16, Mr. Roosevelt said:

The World Economic Conference . . . must establish order in place of the present chaos by the stabilization of currencies, the freeing of the flow of world trade, and international action to raise price levels. It must supplement individual domestic programs for economic recovery by wise, considered international action.

The World Economic Conference met in London on June 12, 1933, and within an hour a troublesome ghost entered. In his opening presidential address, Ramsay MacDonald, the British Prime Minister, referred to the subject of war debts. While admitting that the conference could not consider it, he said it "must be dealt with before every obstacle to general recovery has been removed, and it must be taken up without delay by the nations concerned." The representatives

of other governments voiced the same opinion. This mention of a forbidden subject at once roused resentment in Congress, where some Senators spoke out bitterly. But the plain fact was that the debtor countries, now beginning to default, could not make the required payments without serious further damage to their own currencies, to international exchange, to prices, and to trade, the very things the conference met to improve. The incident served to advertise how and why the conference was crippled.

Getting down to work as best it could under this handicap, the conference tackled the problem of stabilizing the relations between national currencies. This was fundamental, for no matter what else was done there could be no restoration of international trade so long as the relative value of national currencies jumped about in an unpredictable manner. The immediate trouble arose from the abandonment of the gold standard by Great Britain and the United States. How was it possible to do business between these two countries, or between either of them and France, when there was no fixed relation between the values of the American dollar, the British pound, both paper, and the French gold franc? The problem before the conference did not seem too difficult for it to solve, because at the very outset there was a pretty general basis of agreement. The American government had repeatedly expressed the hope of ultimately returning to gold, and had also repeatedly urged immediate stabilization by the conference of national currencies that were not on gold. The British stand was much the same; and the gold bloc countries, while fearful of being forced off their solid standard, were for that very reason all the more anxious to peg the paper currencies.

On June 16, as a first and easy step toward a solution, the American and British experts at the conference drew up a plan to tie the pound and the dollar together temporarily at the current rate of exchange. The next step, which was to tie them to the gold currencies, was never taken. For almost a week London waited for Washington to approve the first step, and then what came was a veto. This alarmed the gold bloc countries. They feared a drive against their currencies. To reassure them and at the same time to make another effort at stabilization, a declaration was prepared to be issued jointly by them, the United States, and Great Britain. It would affirm their belief that stabilization should be obtained as quickly as possible, that the gold countries would stick to their standard, and that the other two desired ultimately to return to it "under proper conditions." On July 3 an even more decisive veto came from Washington.

What the American government had been demanding, it now rejected! The reason was the apparent success of the domestic program for recovery, an essential feature of which was the government's freedom to change the gold value of the dollar. Stabilization would destroy this freedom and upset the program. The refusal of the United States, by far the strongest national unit in the world economy, made international stabilization by the other members of the conference impossible, and they threw up their hands in despair, because currency stabilization was fundamental to almost everything else on the agenda. Adjournment followed.

THE JOHNSON ACT

The problem of war debts was now proving to be impossible of solution by diplomatic methods. Discussions between the creditor and the debtors continued, but neither side was prepared to make any concession that the other could consider. Since payment in full was even more out of the question, the only alternative left was default, which had begun in December, 1932, and became complete in June, 1934, with the negligible exception of Finland. Naturally the reaction in Congress was unpleasant. During the 1933 session, Senator Hiram Johnson introduced a bill to punish the defaulting countries by prohibiting anyone in the United States, under penalty of heavy fine or imprisonment, from buying or selling any of their bonds. It was an extreme measure that would have hit countless Americans who had invested in such securities.

Nevertheless, the bill was dropped only as the result of objections by the Department of State, and it was revived in January, 1934, amended to satisfy the Department of State so that it would not apply to bonds that were then in existence. Its passage was a foregone conclusion. "The slightest intimation from any important source that a revision of the debt settlement was desirable, even in the selfish interest of the United States, evoked bellows of rage from members of Congress." The adoption of this Johnson Act in April, 1934, did a lot of harm and very little, if any, good. For one thing, it hastened the completion of default. Only "token" payments were then being received from any country save Finland, and now these all stopped, the governments that had been making them finding that they might as well pay nothing on account. Secondly, it raised a new obstacle to international loans. Much worse was a third evil. The passage of the Johnson Act was an outburst of national bad temper that embittered international relations.

RECOGNITION OF SOVIET RUSSIA

Negotiations with Russia were also upset by this act. The United States, following the rest of the world, had at last recognized Russia in November, 1933. The first contacts were made at the World Economic Conference, when Maxim Litvinoff, the Russian Commissar for Foreign Affairs, conferred with the American delegation; and shortly afterward Russian purchases of American cotton were financed by a loan that the Reconstruction Finance Corporation gave to the American exporters. Then, on the invitation of President Roosevelt, President Kalinin sent Mr. Litvinoff to Washington to arrange for the establishment of regular diplomatic relations between the two countries, and this was done after only a few days' discussions.

The American recognition of the Soviet government was based on an agreement that was mainly political, the most important part of it being the pledge of each government not to interfere in the internal affairs of the other, which meant that the Soviet government gave its word not to support communistic activities in this country. But the public interest was chiefly concerned with the economic results of recognition. There were good reasons for believing that Russia was anxious to buy enormous quantities of American goods if the necessary credits could be provided. Yet this rich trade was still beyond reach, for there was a long-standing Russian debt problem, the settlement of which was left for negotiations to be undertaken after recognition.

These negotiations were begun in Moscow by Ambassador Bullitt early in 1934, and they proved very difficult. There were private claims of American citizens for property confiscated in Russia, and there was a world of difference between the old American and the new Russian concepts of private property. The United States also claimed that the Soviet government was responsible for a war loan advanced to the short-lived Kerensky regime of 1917. This was denied, as well it might be, for the great Russian revolution had intervened, and intelligent Russians knew that much of the disputed loan had been spent on fighting the Soviet regime in its beginning. A compromise might have been reached, based on the granting of new credits to Russia, if the Johnson Act had not been passed. This obstructed the development of a trade that was much desired because it would stimulate American production. . . .

AN IMPROVED LATIN AMERICAN POLICY

The greatest contribution the United States had ever made to the improvement of international relations, however, was the Good Neighbor policy, and to this policy the Roosevelt administration gave early and serious attention. It was most fitting that we should make this particular contribution; for it spread a new spirit in the New World, chasing out an evil spirit that we ourselves had put there.

For about a quarter of a century, beginning with the Spanish-American War, our policy toward Latin America made its people distrust, fear, and even hate us. This is not surprising if we look at ourselves as they saw us during that period. Their catalogue of the imperialist crimes we then committed contains such items as the following: we robbed Spain of Cuba, Puerto Rico, and the Philippines; we pretended to give Cuba to the Cubans but really established an American protectorate over that island by means of the Platt Amendment; we grabbed the Canal

Zone by engineering in Colombia the revolution that set up the new state of Panama; Theodore Roosevelt's congressional message, often called the "Roosevelt Corollary" to the Monroe Doctrine, bluntly warned the Latin American states to behave, which meant to do what we wanted, or we would make them; because they did not pay their debts, we forcibly entered the Dominican Republic, Haiti, and Nicaragua—and we stayed there, managing their finances and other governmental affairs.

We began definitely to mend our ways in the twenties, during the Coolidge and Hoover administrations. In 1924, we withdrew our armed forces from the Dominican Republic, though we continued to collect its customs and to turn over part of the proceeds to its creditors. Our military occupation of Nicaragua was broken for a while in 1925–1926. When the government of Mexico confiscated oil properties belonging to our citizens, our government did not dispatch troops and ships to protect them but offered to arbitrate, and sent a new ambassador, Dwight Morrow, who displayed a sympathetic understanding of Mexico's difficult problems. His arrival in Mexico in the fall of 1927 marked the beginning of much friendlier relations between the two countries. At the Havana Conference of 1928, to allay some lively Latin American suspicions about the presence of our forces in Haiti and Nicaragua, one of the delegates of our government announced: "We have no desire to stay. We entered to meet an imperative but temporary emergency, and we shall retire as soon as possible."

Immediately after this conference, the Department of State prepared an important memorandum on the Monroe Doctrine, which was finally published in 1930. This repudiated the so-called Roosevelt Corollary as an improper interpretation of the doctrine, and conveyed the assurance that the doctrine would not again be used, because it could not, to justify American armed intervention in the domestic affairs of Latin American countries. The promise was kept, though American bondholders suffered by the default of two Latin American governments in 1932. In the beginning of January, 1933, following a general election in Nicaragua, the last of our marines departed from that country according to a pledge that had been given by Secretary of State Stimson.

The policy thus begun owes its striking name and its greatest development to President F. D. Roosevelt. In his inaugural address on March 4, 1933, he dedicated this country to the policy of the "Good Neighbor"—"who resolutely respects himself and, because he does so, respects the rights of others—the neighbor who respects his obligations and respects the sanctity of his agreements in and with world neighbors." The new administration was at once put to the test by revolutionary outbursts in Cuba. Mr. Roosevelt steadfastly refused to intervene to restore order, though he was urged to do so by many Cubans as well as Americans and though he might have done so under the Platt Amendment. Instead, he sent a special envoy to bring the warring factions together, he offered American aid to relieve the severe economic distress that was largely responsible for the political disturbances, and he consulted with the strongest Latin American states on how to handle the unpleasant crisis. . . .

Early in 1934 we recognized the new government in Cuba, but not before President Roosevelt discussed the matter with representatives of seventeen Latin American states at a White House conference. A few months later our protectorate over the island was ended by the abrogation of the Platt Amendment, which occasioned a three-day celebration in Cuba and caused the heads of various Latin American governments to send appreciative messages to Washington. By the end of the summer the first trade agreement was signed—with Cuba. The same summer saw the withdrawal of our marines from Haiti, and in the following year we surrendered our financial control of its government, the terms of the transfer having been ratified by a plebiscite of the people of Haiti. Also in 1935, by the most punctilious cooperation with South American governments, we succeeded in stopping the Chaco war between Bolivia and Paraguay, which for five years had defied attempts at pacification. In 1936, we completed negotiations to give up treaty rights in Panama that were similar to those we had possessed in Cuba under the Platt Amendment.

A special conference to consider how the peace of the Americas could best be guarded was suggested by President Roosevelt in January, 1936, and after ten months of careful preparations it met in Buenos Aires. He went there in person to open it, the first President of the United States ever to visit South America while in office. His appearance and his speech electrified Latin America. He spoke for the whole of the New World, something no man had ever been able to do before. The distrust with which the United States had long been regarded in Central and South America was now almost entirely gone, having been removed in the only possible way, by the considerate action of our own government over a period of years. Now the states of the Pan American Union, no longer dominated by us, joined in a consultative pact to give solidity to their common desire to preserve the peace. They pledged one another to consult together in the event of war or the threat of war and also whenever any nation should attempt to intervene in their affairs. Our Good Neighbor policy was at last binding the New World together.

WORLD PEACE BREAKS DOWN

The year 1935 marked a great shift of emphasis from domestic problems to international ones. Until then our outlook was dominated by the depression that had gripped us. Of course we knew the rest of the world was also struggling with it, but we were not much concerned by what was happening in other countries. We had enough worries of our own right at home, and they largely governed our foreign policy. We sought international cooperation, or turned our backs upon it, according as we thought it would aid or retard our own economic recovery. We were climbing up, with prosperity as our goal. Then the whole view changed, as conditions in the rest of the world began to point unmistakably to another world war. Peace supplanted prosperity as our goal, and international problems replaced domestic ones as the controlling influence over our foreign policy. We were determined to stay out of war. But how? That was the great question, and there was no answer that convinced the whole nation. We continued to shun international cooperation, or to seek it, in the degree to which we thought it would keep us out of war.

The world conditions that caused this shift were more or less terrifying, for the foundations of international law and order crumbled before our eyes. The crumbling had really begun four years before in Manchuria when Japan flagrantly violated the League Covenant, the Nine-

Power Treaty, and the Kellogg Pact. She was able to do it because the forces behind international law and order were so paralyzed that they could do nothing to stop her. Then the fatal weakness of our international society was exposed. Most Westerners, however, did not seem to think this weakness mattered very much to them, appearing as it did in that distant region of the earth—and that is why it appeared there. Moreover, few of us took Japan seriously in those days. But we were thoroughly alarmed when the foundations of peace were overturned in Europe. There, we had rather innocently supposed, no Power would dare to follow Japan's example of lawlessness, for the rest would have to pull together quickly to stop it for their own safety. We knew there were strains and stresses in the Old World, but we took it for granted that they could somehow be adjusted. The Ethiopian crisis shattered our illusion in 1935.

We have already traced the frantic efforts made in Europe, particularly by France, to strengthen fences after Germany announced her withdrawal from the League in the autumn of 1933. (See pp. 234 ff.) France had negotiated a pact of mutual assistance with Russia; Russia had also been welcomed by the Western Powers as a member of the League and given a seat on the Council. In further search of reinforcement, France had negotiated her agreement of January, 1935, with Italy, settling their outstanding differences. Nothing had been gained, however. In March, 1935, Germany had increased the uneasiness by adopting conscription and beginning to rearm in defiance of the Versailles Treaty. In the early months of the same year, Mussolini, shrewdly taking advantage of the fear that he might go over to Germany, had

pressed on with his obvious preparations to attack Ethiopia. Nor had he been restrained even by the suggestion of Britain and France that Italian desires for expansion in Africa should be satisfied by some measure of concession. The shipment of war materials for an Ethiopian campaign had continued unabated.

By the summer of 1935 the outlook was dark. On July 10, Secretary Hull called in the Italian ambassador and informed him that the United States was deeply interested in preserving the peace in all parts of the world, was increasingly concerned over Italy's dispute with Ethiopia, and earnestly hoped for a mutually satisfactory settlement of it. Then on August 18, President Roosevelt sent a personal message to Mussolini stating that the government and the people of the United States felt that failure to reach a peaceful settlement and a resort to hostilities would be a world calamity the consequences of which would injure the interests of all nations.

This appeal followed immediately upon a move to back up American words with American action that would uphold the League in its efforts to bring Italy to reason. On the previous day the chairman of the House Committee on Foreign Affairs introduced a joint resolution, drafted with the aid of experts in the Department of State, giving the President discretionary power to impose an arms embargo on one or all of the belligerents in the event of war and to take other action to preserve the peace. It was now quite clear that the League was about to try sanctions, the success or failure of which might turn on whether we supported them or not. Almost at once there was a great American stampede in the opposite direction, and Congress quickly tied the President's hands so that he could not cooperate with European efforts to preserve the peace.

THE NEUTRALITY ACT OF 1935

The panicky passage of the Neutrality Law of August, 1935, was the sudden climax of a strong national belief that our entry into the last war had been an awful blunder and that we should never repeat it. Why had we made the mistake? The popular answer then was that we had been tricked by propaganda, foreign and domestic, and betrayed by selfish interests, particularly the international bankers and the munition-makers. For over a year, probably as a result of the failure of the international movement for disarmament, the public of this country had been roused by books and magazine articles exposing the diabolically clever intrigues and the horribly fat profits of the European "merchants of death," the private manufacturers of the implements of war. More authoritative and no less sensational were the revelations made by Senator Nye's committee, whose public hearings had begun in September, 1934, and whose report was to be completed in 1936. As a result, hosts of people were convinced that the private traffic in arms was the main cause of war. Early in 1935, Congress was presented with nearly a score of bills to prevent the United States from being sucked into "the next war." They relied on such devices as taking the profits out of war, prohibiting the sale of munitions to belligerents or the granting of bank credits to them, and forbidding Americans to travel in war zones.

When the war scare burst upon the country in August, the Senate took the bit in its teeth and rushed through a joint resolution imposing a mandatory embargo on the shipment of war materials to all belligerents. This was carrying out the threat that the Senate Foreign Relations Committee had made in 1933 during the Disarmament Conference. Now the leaders of the House, who preferred the administration policy, objected to the Senate resolution, forcing a compromise that became law. The mandatory embargo was to continue only until the end of February, and the President was given discretionary authority to prohibit Americans' traveling on ships of belligerent countries except at their own risk, and to bar belligerent submarines from our waters. As Congress was expressing the undoubted will of the mass of the nation, the President could only utter a warning, when he signed the bill, that a rigid arms embargo "might drag us into war instead of keeping us out."

THE ETHIOPIAN CRISIS

For some months Europe trembled on the brink of war. In September the British fleet was concentrated in the Mediterranean, and Mussolini rejected the League's final plan for a settlement and raised his army to one million men. In the beginning of October he launched his attack on Ethiopia, the League formally condemned him and proceeded to apply sanctions, and President Roosevelt promptly imposed the embargo. The President also warned Americans not to travel on belligerent ships; and, in addition, he stated that "any of our people who voluntarily engage in transactions of any character with either of the belligerents do so at their own risk."

Because we happened to have practically no trade with Ethiopia, the law operated against Italy by prohibiting the export of "arms, ammunition, and implements of war," and we were glad because we sympathized with the victim of aggression. But if export of these things was prohibited, why not also that of many other supplies that could be used for military purposes? If we did not stop the flow of these things too, we should still be aiding Italy to conquer Ethiopia in defiance of the League and its sanctions, and we should be making profit out of it, in violation of the spirit though not the letter of the law. So the administration tried to discourage the country from doing business with Italy. The first step was the warning, already mentioned, not to expect government support, and this was followed by other appeals. Secretary Hull, for example, announced his conviction that the American people opposed "war profits at the expense of human lives and misery." But exports swelled to meet the Italian demand, and on November 15, Mr. Hull was more outspoken. Commodities such as oil, copper, trucks, tractors, scrap iron and scrap steel, which are essentially war materials although not actually arms, ammunition or implements of war," he then pointed out, were being shipped from here in considerably increased quantities "directly contrary to the policy of this government" and "the general spirit of the recent Neutrality Act."

The attempt to discourage a trade that the law permitted was a failure, and it was resented by Italy. On November 22, the Italian ambassador, under orders from his government, called on Mr. Hull and lodged a protest. He said that though our government's statements theoretically applied to both sides, it was well known that they applied practically only to Italy, that this constituted a violation of the Italo-American treaty of 1781 and was an "unfriendly act." Mr. Hull replied that it was impossible to understand how Italy could go to war in violation of the Kellogg Pact and then claim that we must supply her with materials of war or be guilty of an unfriendly act, and he insisted that it was the United States that

had a real complaint against Italy for disturbing the peace of the world. Much more serious than this diplomatic tiff was the effect of our private pursuit of profit in this undeclared war against Ethiopia. The failure to check the swelling stream of American oil and other war supplies pouring into Italy was alone sufficient to dissuade the League Powers from proceeding from partial sanctions, which had been applied, to full sanctions. This, however, was not their only reason. Mussolini intimated that full sanctions meant war, and the League Powers were not prepared to fight Italy to save Ethiopia, which was overrun in 1936. . . .

THE NEUTRALITY ACT OF 1936

There were high debates in Congress between the opening of the session on January 3, 1936, and the last day of February, when the temporary law was due to expire. The President broke a precedent by delivering his opening message in the evening, so that the nation could hear it on the radio, and he devoted most of his attention to the terrible international situation. He deplored "the temper and the purposes of the rulers of many of the great populations in Europe and in Asia." The people of the world wanted peace, he said, but they were being frustrated by 10 or 15 per cent of their number, who had impatiently "reverted to the old belief in the law of the sword, or to the fantastic conception that they, and they alone, are chosen to fulfill a mission, and that all the others among the billion and a half of human beings must and shall learn from them and be subject to them." On the same day an administration bill was introduced into the two houses. It preserved the mandatory embargo on arms, munitions, and implements of war, and empowered the President to extend it at his discretion to prohibit the export of other articles or materials used "in the conduct of war" over and above what had been exported in peace time. It also prohibited loans and credits to belligerent governments, and permitted the President to put Americans on their own risk when doing business with any belligerent.

The more this bill was debated, the more impossible did it seem to work out a permanent measure in the short time allowed, with the result that the expiring temporary measure was renewed till May, 1937, with three amendments. The first forbade loans to belligerents. This had little practical value, since the Johnson Act of 1934 had closed the American bond market to such countries as would be likely to seek loans for war purposes. The second amendment extended the mandatory embargo to states that joined a war after it had started. This plugged a hole in the original law, and was a warning against the application of military sanctions by the League. The third amendment exempted from the operation of the law American republics at war with non-American states unless they were cooperating with non-American states in the prosecution of the war. This plugged another hole, one that might betray the Monroe Doctrine.

THE SPANISH CIVIL WAR

The Neutrality Act of 1936 was signed on February 28, and within five months the crisis for which it was framed had passed away and was succeeded by another crisis of such a different character that it made a mockery of our law. This was the outbreak of the Spanish civil war. Fascist Italy and Nazi Germany intervened to support Franco in destroying the Spanish Republic, while Communist Russia intervened to preserve it. There

were grave fears that this struggle might soon embroil all Europe unless it were stopped; but opinion in France and Great Britain was so divided in sympathy, as it was in this country, that all the governments of those two Powers could do was to try to get a European agreement to prevent the sending of aid to either side in the Spanish conflict.

This war was as bad as the one in Ethiopia, but the Neutrality Act did not apply. It dealt with wars between nations and had nothing to say about civil wars. Now the President had no discretionary power to stop exports to the belligerents, and Congress, which had insisted on tying his hands, was not in session. He could not cooperate with the other nations in imposing an honest neutrality, nor could he use anything but moral suasion to prevent shipments of arms to the factions fighting in Spain. He used this, however, and got loyal cooperation until the end of the year, when an American citizen insisted on his legal right to send a consignment of airplanes and engines. The members of Congress were dismayed, but when they met on January 6, 1937, they found it impossible to extend the law to cover civil wars. How was a civil war to be defined so as to distinguish it from an insurrection? Each case would have to be decided according to the circumstances, and this meant giving discretion to the President, which Congress would not countenance. So a joint resolution was hurried through both houses, making the law apply in this particular case. A special law for Spain! It fitted in with the European nonintervention agreement. But as the Spanish strife continued and it became apparent that this agreement was being flagrantly violated, our nonintervention was severely criticized by American sympathizers with each side, and there was pressure to get the law changed. The administration, however, believed that a change would not serve the cause of peace and might lead to our being involved. Congress was content to leave it alone.

THE "CASH AND CARRY" ACT

On May 1, 1937, the day when the Neutrality Act was due to expire, it was replaced by a "permanent" measure, which retained the mandatory embargo on arms, munitions, and implements of war, and also the prohibition on loans to belligerents. In addition, it included a formula to cover civil wars; it forbade American travel on belligerent ships, which was no longer to be allowed at the individuals' risk; and it prohibited the arming of American merchant ships, that there might be no question of their innocence. A further feature of the new law was so controversial that this was not made permanent like the rest but was enacted for only two years. It had been strongly argued that the ban on arms, munitions, and implements of war was illogical because these were not the only contraband of war, and that we should either lift the ban on these few articles or extend it to everything else that belligerents could use for war purposes. The argument was unanswerable, but we were in no mood to be logical. The lifting of the ban would violate the national conscience, whereas the extension of the ban would work great injury on the country as a whole by outlawing a most profitable trade. But trade with belligerents might get us into their wars. To avoid this danger, the device of "cash and carry" was adopted. This imposed two restrictions on the export of non-embargoed goods to belligerents. They

were not to be carried in American ships, and before they left the country they had to be fully paid for in cash. This provision was to last until May 1, 1939.

JAPAN RUNS AMUCK

As Italy and Germany profited by the example of Japan, and assisted each other to do it, Japan in turn took advantage of the disturbances they created. Late in 1935, while the Western Powers were distracted by the crisis in Europe, Japan launched an "autonomy movement" of her own to rob China of her northern provinces. This fresh aggression in the Far East moved Secretary Hull on December 5 to make a public statement emphasizing the interest of the United States in the preservation of peace there as elsewhere and the necessity "in this period of world-wide political unrest and economic instability that governments and peoples keep faith in principles and pledges."

In about a fortnight the mask was lifted from the face of Japan. It was done in Tokyo by a high official of the Japanese Foreign Office, Saburo Kurusu, who was to play a treacherous role in 1941. In a conversation with a member of our embassy staff on December 23, 1935, Kurusu stated that Japan was destined to be the leader of Oriental civilization and would in time be the "boss" of "China, India, the Netherlands East Indies, etc." Our destiny, according to him, was to lead Occidental civilization, for Great Britain was "degenerating" and Russia would never "amount to anything." In short, we should agree to divide the world between us. He insisted that our two countries should never fight each other, for that would be suicidal.

Three weeks later, on January 15, 1936, the Japanese delegation walked out of a naval conference in London because the other Powers would not grant her parity, and without it she refused to be bound by the existing treaty limitations when they should expire at the end of the year. As the chairman of the American delegation remarked, "naval parity would give to Japan naval superiority"; and Japan was determined to have naval superiority in the Far East in order that she might be supreme in that part of the world. The signature of the Anti-Comintern Pact in the following November was an indication that Japan, finding it impossible to get our cooperation, would work in partnership with Germany.

The major war that many people were expecting Japan to launch against China began with a battle between Japanese and Chinese forces at the famous Marco Polo Bridge near Peiping, the ancient capital of China, on the night of July 7–8, 1937. As the fighting spread and the seriousness of the situation became apparent, which was within a week, there were consultations between Washington and London. Our stake in the crisis was not only our general interest in the maintenance of peace and our particular interest in the preservation of the Open Door in China, which Japan had slammed shut in Manchuria, but also the lives of American civilians and the safety of American forces that, under old treaties, were stationed in the combat zone. This crisis therefore threatened to involve us in war as none of the preceding crises had done. The danger, which one might think would have made us more disposed to international cooperation, had precisely the opposite effect. It intensified the isolationist feeling that had seized the country, and this to such a degree that our government had to exercise the greatest caution to avoid even the appearance of acting in concert with other governments.

It is doubtful, however, if we could have gained anything by seeking cooperation, for our paralysis coincided with the paralysis of the European Powers that might have worked with us in an effort to restrain Japan. They were living from day to day in mortal terror lest the strife raging in Spain, well described as a "little world war," suddenly set the whole of the Old World aflame.

AMERICAN PROTESTS

Secretary Hull remonstrated with the Japanese ambassador on July 12, pointing out the futility of war and its awful consequences, emphasizing the fact that victor as well as vanquished must suffer. He said he had been looking forward to an early time when Japan and the United States would have an opportunity for world leadership with a constructive program to restore and preserve peace and prosperity. On the same day Secretary Morgenthau signed an agreement with the Finance Minister of China for American aid in stabilizing the Chinese currency, but this had been negotiated before the crisis. Four days later Mr. Hull issued a statement of fundamental principles of international policy as conceived by our government. It was framed in the most general terms, without any reference to the conflict in China. We stood for peace, national and international restraint, abstinence from force and interference in other people's affairs, faithful observance of treaties and their revision by peaceful negotiation when necessary, strengthening of international law, economic security and stability the world over, freer trade, reduction of armaments, and cooperation with other governments, but no entangling alliances or commitments. The last point is interesting in light of the fact that China had just appealed to us and to more than a dozen other countries under the League Covenant, the Nine-Power Treaty, and the Kellogg Pact.

Opinion in Tokyo interpreted the statement as meaning that we had changed our Far Eastern policy since the Manchurian crisis. The statement was circulated among the other governments of the world for comment, and of course they all agreed, even the governments of Germany, Italy, and Japan. The last added, however, that the application of these principles in the Far East had to take into account the particular circumstances of that region.

Our appeals for peace, which were repeated, were not the only ones addressed by Western Powers to Japan, but words could make no impression upon her. We offered our good offices, as did Great Britain, to assist in effecting a settlement with China, but Japan made no response. Our helplessness sprang from no lack of understanding by the government of what Japan was aiming at. From August, 1937, Secretary Hull proceeded, as he told the Canadian minister a year later, on the theory that "Japan definitely contemplates securing domination over as many hundreds of millions of people as possible in eastern Asia and gradually extending her control through the Pacific islands to the Dutch East Indies and elsewhere, thereby dominating in practical effect that one-half of the world."

The Neutrality Act was not applied, and for very good reasons. Though Japan was undoubtedly making war, she declared she was not. Therefore there was legally no war until the President proclaimed that it existed. After several White House conferences, the administration reached the conclusion, concurred in by the nation, that at least for the time being it was better not to invoke the law. The contrast with our attitude of a year

before is striking. Then we were eager to apply the law to Spain when it could not be applied, and now we would not apply it to the Far East when we could. We feared that the law, thanks to its rigidity, would aid the aggressor—the very opposite of what it had done in the Ethiopian crisis. The embargo of arms, munitions, and implements of war would hurt China much more than Japan, for the manufacture of these things was as great in Japan as it was small in China. As for other supplies, of which Japan as well as China stood in great need, Japan could get all and China none if we invoked the law. Then Japan, by declaring war, could establish a legal blockade of the whole Chinese coast, shutting off all supplies, while she, possessing a large mercantile marine, could come and get all she wanted under our "cash and carry" regulation.

ROOSEVELT'S "QUARANTINE" SPEECH

The League of Nations, having had its back broken in wrestling with the Ethiopian crisis, could do little in response to China's appeal. It sent a futile protest, similar to ours, to Japan against the bombing of noncombatant areas; and on October 5 it passed judgment on Japan as an aggressor, calling upon the signatories of the Nine-Power Treaty to assemble and consider how to stop the Sino-Japanese War. It was "passing the buck" to a definite group of interested Powers of which we were looked upon as the leader, and on this very day President Roosevelt delivered his startling "quarantine" speech in Chicago. The coincidence was obviously no mere accident. Though he named no names, everybody knew that his scathing denunciation of "war-makers" included not only Japan but also Germany and Italy. Isolation and neutrality, he boldly said, offered no real protection. Referring to what had come to pass in other parts of the world, he warned:

Let no one imagine that America will escape, that America may expect mercy, that this western hemisphere will not be attacked and that it will continue tranquilly and peacefully to carry on the ethics and the arts of civilization. . . . If we are to have a world in which we can breathe freely and live in amity without fear, the peace-loving nations must make a concerted effort to uphold laws and principles on which peace can rest secure. . . .

War is a contagion, whether it be declared or undeclared. It can engulf states and peoples remote from the original scene of hostilities. We are determined to keep out of war, yet we cannot insure ourselves against the disastrous effect of war and the dangers of involvement. We are adopting such measures as will minimize the risk of involvement, but we cannot have complete protection in a world of disorder in which confidence and security have broken down.

He would "quarantine" aggressors. His words were a courageous effort to rally American opinion behind international cooperation, but the country was more than ever afraid that our government would drag us into war. Incidentally the Japanese ambassador called to inquire what the President meant by "quarantine." . . .

[Despite adverse criticism of his speech, Roosevelt,] in his budget message to Congress on January 5, 1938, . . . called for an increase of 8 per cent in the appropriations for the army and the navy, which was not out of line with the votes of the immediately preceding years, but he was careful to add that he might have to ask for more later. He did it before the month was out. A fortnight after the defeat of the war referendum, he requested an addition of 20 per cent of the authorized naval building program. Hitherto our plans had kept within the limits of the Washington and London treaties, but this meant going beyond, and the new departure in naval policy stirred heated debates. Isolationists fought hard against it, arguing that our present force was adequate for defense and that any more would be courting war, but they lacked the votes to match their words. Still the strength of their opposition was reflected in the fact that whereas only fifteen members of the House voted against the normal naval appropriations, there were a hundred against this supplementary measure. Since 1932 most of our navy had been in the Pacific. Now it was openly admitted that we should keep it there and, in addition, develop an Atlantic fleet. There was a growing recognition that war might burst upon us out of Europe as well as out of the Far East. We were turning from weakness to strength.

HITLER ON THE MARCH

The shadow cast by Hitler on the world grew very big and black in 1938, confirming the opinion already formed in Secretary Hull's mind, that Germany was "bent on becoming the dominating colossus of continental Europe" as Japan was bent upon ruling Eastern Asia. In March of this year, Nazi forces rolled into terrorized Austria and its annexation to Germany was proclaimed. Europe trembled, and Mr. Hull seized the occasion for some plain speaking to the American people.

The address delivered in Washington by the Secretary of State on March 17, just a few days after this outrage, was a bold challenge to the nation. The momentous question before us, he said, was whether the doctrine of naked force would again be enthroned in the world or whether the United States and other peaceful nations would work together to preserve law, order, morality, and justice as the basic principles of international society. He pointed out that we could, if we chose, turn our backs on the whole problem but that such a choice would entail great sacrifices. If we let other nations see that we would not defend our legitimate interests abroad but would abandon them at the first sign of danger, our international relations would shrink until we became "a self-constituted hermit state." This would mean reorganizing our entire social, economic, and political structure, reducing our standard of living, and submitting to regimentation. Even if we did all this to avoid war, still we should not be safe. We might refuse to participate in world affairs but, he added, "we cannot thereby withdraw from the world itself." Instead of being "a means of security," isolation was "a fruitful means of insecurity." Our own selfish interest required us to cooperate with others in establishing world order based on law.

These were brave words, but they offered no solution of a puzzling problem that the fall of Austria forced upon our government. Should we apply the Stimson Doctrine, or should we recognize the Nazi annexation of what was, after all, a German country? We had a trade agreement with Austria, and Germany was on our "blacklist." Recognition meant putting Austria on the "blacklist." On the other hand, nonrecognition, which would continue our most-favored-nation treatment of Austrian goods, would allow German goods to gain the same advantage by being exported through Austria. Then there was the question of the debt that had been contracted by Austria under international arrangements in the early twenties to put that country on its feet. It was still being serviced. If we

maintained the fiction that Austria was still an independent state, our share of the loan would be a fiction too. Though this was too small an item to have much weight in determining our course, which was to recognize what had happened, the debt became an irritant. A Washington note to Berlin stating that the United States looked to Germany to discharge Austria's debt evoked a denial of responsibility. The German Minister of Economics even gave us a lecture for demanding payment when we had not honored the Confederate debt after the Civil War. Berlin then proceeded to conclude agreements with nearly all the creditor countries for partial payment on Austrian bonds, but would make no such concession to the United States. This higgling over the debt, however, was as nothing compared with the reign of terror that had started in Europe with the seizure of Austria. The Nazi mechanized legions had burst the bounds of their own land. They were on the march, and everyone could see what country was marked as the next victim.

THE MUNICH CRISIS

The strong defenses that Czechoslovakia had built along the mountain border separating her from Germany were turned by the annexation of Austria, and by the same stroke she found herself almost surrounded by the Nazi Reich. How soon would the jaws of the monster close on the little state it would devour? When Hitler immediately launched a war of nerves against Prague, raising the devil among the Sudeten Germans, opinion in this country was much more concerned than it had been over the fate of Austria. Czechoslovakia was recognized as a sort of foster child of the United States, and we had another good reason for taking a lively interest in it at this particular time.

Because Czechoslovakia was the bulwark of democracy in Central Europe, and both France and Russia were pledged to defend it against aggression, we could see that a Nazi assault upon it might suddenly kindle the flames of the war that we were all dreading.

To anxious American eyes, the Second World War seemed very close in May, when the Czechs leaped to arms in response to German military maneuvers just across the border. Though the immediate crisis passed, we did not know that Hitler then, as he later boasted, "ordered that preparations should be made for military action against this state by October 2." As the summer wore on, the war of nerves increased in intensity, coming to a head in the crisis of September, when Germany seemed all ready to strike. France was calling out her army, and Britain had mobilized her fleet. We knew that Mr. Chamberlain nearly despaired of preserving peace when he, who had never trusted himself to an airplane before, flew three times to Germany. "If at first you don't succeed, fly, fly again," said a caustic wit afterward. Until the third trip, it was almost impossible to see how a great war could be avoided.

When the British Prime Minister was making desperate appeals not only to Hitler but also to President Beneš, we joined in the chorus. On September 26, President Roosevelt sent personal messages to the heads of the governments of Czechoslovakia, France, Germany, and Great Britain urging a peaceful settlement. Later in the day he received their replies. Only Germany's was unfavorable, Hitler making it clear that he must have the Sudetenland right away and would take it by force if necessary. On the next day, Mr. Roosevelt sent a second appeal to Hitler and one to Mussolini. Two days later, Mr. Chamberlain made his third flight, this time to Munich, where he and the French Prime Minister met Hitler and Mussolini and they reached their famous, or infamous, accord by which the Sudetenland was handed over to Germany.

We were startled and angered. Hitler had won another bloodless victory, and it was of prime strategic value to him. He had captured the great natural fortress of Czechoslovakia that barred his path of conquest. He had alienated Russia from France and Great Britain by forcing Paris and London to come to terms behind the back of Moscow. He had inflicted a humiliating defeat on France and Great Britain because he was ready to fight, and they were not. Though they were feverishly arming, it looked as if they might lose the war before it began, if they had not actually lost it already. That this was what they had done was widely suspected in the United States, and many Americans loudly condemned them for not being willing to fight. . . .

MORE SEIZURES

The European situation grew steadily worse through the fall and winter of 1938–1939; and we knew it well, for our foreign radio and press correspondents were keeping us better informed than we had ever been of developments abroad. We saw the civil war in Spain, which cost one and a half million lives, draw to a tragic close, with the victory of Franco, another triumph for the Nazi-Fascist cause.

But we were more disturbed over what Hitler would do next. His appetite grew by what it fed on. He was torturing what was left of helpless Czechoslovakia after Munich, sending more than a hundred ultimatums to Prague before March 15, 1939, when he suddenly forced its abject surrender. Less than a week afterwards, he grabbed the district of Memal from Lithuania; and at the very same time he presented "proposals" to Poland, upon whose government he had been bringing pressure to bear, to agree to the German annexation of Danzig and a strip of territory across the Polish Corridor to East Prussia. We expected Poland to be next on the list; but we were surprised by Mussolini, who celebrated Good Friday, April 7, by pouncing on little Albania. It was a dastardly deed, and yet it did not seem to matter very much. We knew that Nazi Germany, not Fascist Italy, was creating the reign of terror that gripped the Old World.

ROOSEVELT CHALLENGES HITLER

Already the rape of Czechoslovakia had driven Great Britain and France together in a desperate resolve to stop Hitler no matter what the cost might be, and they made no secret of their determination to fight him as soon as he struck at Poland. They knew neither the day nor the hour when the blow would fall, but they were pretty sure it could not be far off, and they speeded their preparations. Great Britain adopted conscription, which she had never done before in time of peace; both the British and the French governments pledged their assistance to Poland, Greece, and Rumania against attack; and they tried to form a united front with Russia against the European monster.

Our President at once spoke out. On April 14 he addressed the Governing Board of the Pan American Union in no uncertain terms but without mentioning names. Referring to Mussolini's recent complaint that his country was a "prisoner" of the Mediterranean, and Hitler's denunciation of the British and French pledges to Poland as a "threat" and an "encirclement," he pointedly remarked

that "there is no such thing as encircling, or threatening, or imprisoning any peaceful nation by other peaceful nations." He also clearly referred to Hitler's shouting for *Lebensraum* when he asked, "Do we really have to assume that nations can find no better methods of realizing their destinies than those which were used by the Huns and the Vandals fifteen hundred years ago?" Later, on this same day, he cabled the two warmongering dictators, putting them on the spot by asking pointblank if they were willing to give assurances that their armed forces would not attack or invade the territory or possessions of any of the independent nations of Europe and the Near East. Copies of the message were given to all other governments, and the appeal was broadcast in six languages. All the world applauded, except the Axis countries. Neither Hitler nor Mussolini replied directly, Hitler giving his answer a fortnight later in a speech to the Reichstag, in which he said that Germany's neighbors knew that Germany had no aggressive designs against them and had received more binding assurances than the President had requested. As if to advertise his brazen duplicity, he announced in this very speech the abrogation of his nonaggression pact with Poland.

Meanwhile the gathering storm was concentrating our attention upon defense measures and neutrality legislation. In his annual message to Congress on January 4, the President said, "All about us grow more deadly armaments," and he observed that the world had become so small and weapons of attack so swift that no nations could be safe "so long as any other single powerful nation refuses to settle its grievances at the council table." Therefore he was convinced that "weapons of defense give the only safety," and he called for more of them. At first the plan was to exceed the appropriations of the previous year by nearly one-third, but before the session ended at midsummer the increase was doubled. Much of the addition was to build up the army air force and to establish new bases. The navy was most anxious to begin building a base in Guam, but Congress rejected this project as liable to provoke Japan, one of the leading isolationists declaring that this was "a direct vote for peace and the most important of its kind in recent years." Congress also provided funds to accumulate stock piles of strategic materials that had to be imported, and the government made a deal with Great Britain to exchange surplus American cotton for surplus British rubber.

DIFFICULTIES OF THE NEUTRALITY LEGISLATION

Neutrality legislation was not such a simple matter as providing money for defense. Experience had amply proved that the law never worked as intended, because circumstances were never the same. It was now well known that American industry had greatly assisted in the rearmament of Germany, whom we regarded as the arch-enemy of peace, thus helping to upset the balance of force in the Old World; and that Great Britain and France, with whom we deeply sympathized in their perilous plight, were buying heavily in this country to redress the balance. On the outbreak of war, the mandatory embargo would prevent them from getting any more airplanes or engines here, even those they had already ordered and paid for. Moreover, Japan would be able to get what they could not, because the law had not been applied to the struggle in the Far East, and we could not apply it there without inflicting a grave injury on China. The same dilemma was raised by the "cash and carry" provision. This would benefit the peace-loving European democracies, which pleased us, but it would equally benefit predatory Japan, which did not please us. An embargo on the export of war materials to Japan would get around this difficulty, but many people feared it would do more harm than good by antagonizing Japan. Then too it would violate our 1911 commercial treaty with Japan. We were in an exasperating tangle. To make matters worse, there was no clear majority of opinion in Congress on what should be done with the law, the views of the members running from the one extreme of total repeal to the opposite extreme of total embargo. The administration wanted a repeal of the mandatory embargo, and a majority of the people seem to have wanted it too. According to the Gallup Poll, the percentage favoring the sale of arms to Great Britain and France in the event of war rose from thirty-four before Munich to fifty-five on March 12, 1939, and to sixty-six four weeks later. In contrast to the mandatory embargo, "cash and carry" had gained public support, but it was only a temporary provision that would expire on May 1, unless extended by that date.

Though the President had criticized the law in his opening message in January, Congress did not approach the task of revising it until roused by the March crisis in Europe. Then conflicting opinions prevented any action by May 1, with the result that the two main features of the law were the very reverse of what the administration and the people desired; for "cash and carry" expired and the arms embargo survived. And this remained the law despite the greatest pressure from the administration. Congress was tired and wanted to go home, while the President, knowing that peace in the

Old World hung by a thread, said he would fight to the finish even if it took all summer. He insisted that the prohibition on the sale of arms to victims of aggression increased the danger of war by suggesting to the menacing dictators that they could do what they liked because the United States would not throw its influence on the side of the democracies to preserve international law and order. This argument only stiffened the backs of the isolationists, and they succeeded in preventing any new legislation until the next session. The Senate Foreign Relations Committee toyed with the idea of terminating the commercial treaty with Japan, and looked forward to dealing with this too at the next session. Then the administration surprised the reluctant legislators by acting on its own, as it had a legal right to do. On July 26, the Department of State sent a note to the Japanese ambassador giving the required six months' notice for the ending of the treaty that tied our hands. Tokyo raged. But Berlin and Rome rejoiced, for the isolationists had continued to play into their hands.

HITLER PLUNGES EUROPE INTO WAR

When Congress adjourned on August 5, 1939, the last obstacle in Hitler's path to war was quietly being removed by the negotiation of the Russo-German nonaggression pact, the announcement of which by the German radio on August 21 burst like a bombshell upon an unsuspecting world. We were dazed. We could not understand what had happened, and we were filled with dark forebodings. Would not Great Britain and France lie down under this terrific defeat by far the worst they had yet suffered? Could Poland do anything but surrender? Had not Hitler won the war without having to fight it? These questions were quickly answered by desperate resolves in London, Paris, and Warsaw.

On the day after the announcement of the Berlin-Moscow pact, Great Britain and France warned Germany that they would fulfill their obligations to Poland just the same, and Poland declared she would fight to defend her independence. The fatal decision was then in Hitler's hands, and all the world knew it. On the following day, August 23, when Ribbentrop flew to Moscow to sign the pact, President Roosevelt sent a personal message to Mussolini to intervene for peace; and on the 24th he appealed directly to Hitler and the President of Poland, asking them to settle their differences by direct negotiation or arbitration or conciliation, and meanwhile to refrain from any hostile action. Poland replied immediately, offering to do as he requested; and on the 25th he sent this reply to Hitler with a further appeal. The only official reply from Germany was a note delivered to the Department of State on the afternoon of September 1, when the Nazi invasion had already begun, stating that Hitler had left nothing untried to effect a friendly settlement with Poland. On the same day Great Britain and France sent an ultimatum to Germany requiring immediate evacuation of Poland, and they followed it with another on the morrow demanding evacuation by noon on the 3rd. When this was not done they too went to war. By way of comment we may quote the following judgment of Professor Sidney B. Fay of Harvard, an outstanding historian and an old friend of Germany: "Never did the ruler of a great state with such mendacity and reckless duplicity plunge it and all Europe into a catastrophe of unforeseeable dimensions, as did Adolf Hitler on September 1."

Stanley G. Payne: THE SECOND SPANISH REPUBLIC, 1931-1939

Stanley G. Payne, who teaches Spanish history at the University of California, Los Angeles, has written Falange, *the first scholarly account of the Fascist movement in Spain. Like Hugh Thomas's six-hundred-page book,* The Spanish Civil War, *Payne's work is an attempt at an objective account of a confused situation. The essay printed below, written for this set of readings, provides a brief history of the Second Spanish Republic.*

SPAIN has been an anachronism in the modern world. After the last of her empire was lost to the United States in 1898, Spain was left—shrunken from her former glory—to face her considerable domestic problems. Twentieth-century Spain, violent, strife-torn, and indecisive, lacked the very structure of a modern nation. Apparently, Spain had been possible only as an empire. By herself, she lacked adequate social institutions, economic development, and the political framework necessary to modern society. Spain was, in the phrase of Ortega y Gasset, "invertebrate."

The first attempt to create a democratic Republic in Spain (1873-74) had been a disaster. The country had been wrenched apart by social rebellion, by attacks from monarchists loyal to the reactionary Carlist faction, and by the regional separatism of the Catalans and Basques. The restored monarchy, which governed Spain in the half century after 1875, had at least preserved civil order and made possible a certain amount of social and economic progress, but national life was dominated by a combination of pressure groups and financial interests vaguely referred to as "the oligarchy." Provincial politics were controlled by a series of rural bosses. Although there was a parliamentary system, elections were never completely fair. Many of the lower class were in misery and had begun to lash out in revolutionary furor. There was no adequate representation of the "national will." The country was so divided into antagonistic social and political groups that there was, in fact, little agreement as to what the "nation" willed.

In such a climate it had not been hard to keep a Republican movement alive. Republicanism gained in prestige as the monarchy degenerated into outright dictatorship in the 1920's. The Republican leaders were middle-class liberals who relied for support on the progressive sectors of the middle-class (about 10 per cent of the population). The majority of the middle and upper-middle class, more conservative in their attitudes, had nonetheless reconciled themselves to a Republican system. The constitutional monarchy was obviously inadequate and a Republican system would provide a moderate alternative to revolutionary upheaval.

The political picture was further complicated by the presence of dissenters committed to more radical goals—the working-class movements and the regional separatists. The principal representatives of the former were the Anarcho-Syndicalists and the Socialists. The

Anarchists, bent on all-out revolution, had been thoroughly squelched by the Monarchist dictatorship of Primo de Rivera. The Socialists, on the other hand, were clever and cooperative. By working with Primo de Rivera's government, they had gained strength during the 1920's. The Anarchists and Socialists together represented the masses; either might have been able to out-vote the middle-class Republican liberals.

The regional separatists were significant in Catalonia and in the Basque country. These two sections were the most industrialized and progressive regions of Spain. They both possessed distinctive local cultures sustained by their own separate languages. Both resented centralized government from Madrid. By 1931, both regions were represented by strong "local nationalist" movements for autonomy in their respective areas.

When municipal elections were held throughout Spain on April 12, 1931, the larger towns voted Republican. It was clear that few Spaniards retained confidence in the monarchy. There had been too much political finagling and corruption, too much social repression, too much obstruction from the king himself. The upper-class was unwilling to defend the monarchy. Even the Spanish army—a ludicrous organization overweighted with hundreds of generals, incapable of modern warfare, used only as a grand national police force—refused to sustain the king. Rather than provoke open war, Alfonso XIII left the country on April 14. The Republic was proclaimed the same day. Full political freedom was restored, but the conservatives were reassured by the liberals who promised that the Republic would be conservative and respectable, a Republic of unity and order.

The elections for a Constitutional Assembly in mid-1931 were the first fully free elections Spain had ever known. In accordance with their revolutionary principles, the Anarchists abstained. Capitalizing on their new prestige, the Republican liberals formed an alliance with the Socialists and won an overwhelming victory.

The Constitutional Assembly proceeded to write a model Republican constitution, as progressive as any in the world. The only part of the document to arouse serious controversy was the sections dealing with the role of the Spanish Catholic Church. The Republican liberals were vehemently anticlerical. The Church in Spain had been strongly tied to the monarchy and the upper class. It was authoritarian and condemned all forms of modern liberalism. The liberals were determined to break the close connection between Church and State, to end State subsidies to the Church, and to remove the Church from Spanish education. These goals were all achieved by the Republican constitution (which also legalized divorce, to the horror of pious Catholics).

Clerical leaders stormed from the Assembly in a huff and laid plans for a new Catholic center party that would rescue control of the Republic from the liberals. Meanwhile, the Republicans turned to the country's next most important institution—the Army. The Spanish officer corps included 600 generals and well over 20,000 officers. It commanded few troops, had little equipment and scant military skill, protected the nation from no foreign enemy (there was none), and consumed an intolerable portion of the national budget. Furthermore, the army had persistently intervened in politics. The liberals wanted to reform the army, to take it out of politics, and to reduce the drain on the treasury. The Minister of War in 1931, the liberal leader Manuel Azaña, tried to reduce the size of the officer corps and to improve the army. His reforms, however, merely encouraged half the officers to retire without changing the basic structure, attitude, or efficiency of the military. The Republican leaders lacked the money, power, and insight to do better. This was their first failure.

The third project of the Republicans, an agrarian reform, never materialized. Spain was basically agrarian and her worst economic problems were caused by rural poverty and backwardness. A sound agrarian reform was imperative to provide peace and justice for Spain. It would also have broken the potentially reactionary power of the great landlords. The difficulty was, however, that the liberals had indulged themselves in an all-out campaign against the Church and never had the time nor energy to deal with the agrarian problem.

The very threat that they might do so, together with the enormous antagonism created among the military by Azaña's reforms, sparked an abortive military rebellion in August, 1932. This was led nominally by General Sanjurjo, an activist very popular among his fellow officers. The revolt failed when most of the officers declined to act. Nonetheless, it was clear that a considerable portion of the military regarded the Republic as their enemy.

To make matters worse, the Republic was attacked from the Left as well as from the Right. The Anarchists, two million strong and the largest single political movement in Spain, had declared the Republic to be but the prelude to their own Anarchist version of "libertarian communism." From the beginning, they had combatted the government and attempted several revolutionary uprisings in different parts of Spain. Their attitude, combined with the bitter antagonism of the clericals, intensified the frustration of the Republican liberals. The Socialists too grew tired of their partnership with the liberals; they left the government, which was then too weak to continue. The second round of elections were held in October, 1933.

By that time the middle-class moderates who had previously voted liberal were disappointed and apprehensive. Deserting *en masse,* they voted for the conservative wing of the Republicans and for the new Catholic federation (known by its initials as the CEDA). The latter attracted most Spanish conservatives, most of the business interests, and the Catholic peasantry of the north. On this basis the CEDA became the largest single party in the new Spanish parliament, but was not able to control the government alone. The Republican president, excluding the Catholics who were set on Church privileges and constitutional changes, made the head of the right-wing Republicans prime minister.

The working-class movements were livid over the conservative victory. The Anarchists continued to plot revolution and the Socialists threatened rebellion should the CEDA be admitted to the government. When several CEDA ministers joined the cabinet in October of 1934, the Socialists revolted. They were joined by the Catalan separatists who had been granted local autonomy but were still unsatisfied. The rebellion in Barcelona—the chief city of Catalonia—was easily repressed, but the miners of the Asturias seized control of their region and were defeated only after an energetic campaign by the regular army. Moorish auxiliaries were brought over from Morocco to help subdue the revolutionaries. There were loudly publicized atrocities on both sides. Lines were drawn as in virtual civil war.

For the next eighteen months, the right-wing Republicans tried desperately to retain control of the government. They hoped to conciliate both sides by leniency to the subversive Left and acquiescence in many of the goals of the Catholic Right. During 1934 and 1935, the original Republican reforms were conveniently forgotten while the State subsidy to the Church was quietly continued. The "black biennium," as these two years were called, constituted a period of governmental stagnation. The right-wing Republicans hoped to soothe violent passions by sitting tight on an explosive mass of class, institutional, and regional antagonisms. Their negative approach was a total failure, for the Republican liberals felt betrayed, the Leftists and separatists defrauded, and the Catholics frustrated.

New elections were held in February of 1936. For this occasion, a "Popular Front" was formed by the Republican liberals, the regionalists, the Socialists, and the insignificantly small Communist Party. The Popular Front's platform was a return to the original program of 1931. Although the Anarchists would not join this "bourgeois" coalition, they permitted their members to vote individually for the Popular Front. The Catholics and conservatives, on the other hand, formed a "National Front" to gain control of the government. Political life was thus sharply polarized around two blocs; the right-wing Republicans were squeezed out.

In the balloting, the Popular Front scored nearly 50 per cent of the popular votes and gained control of parliament. A new government was formed of the Republican liberals led by Azaña. It proposed to do no more than grant complete amnesty to the imprisoned revolutionaries of 1934 and revive the old reforms of five years earlier. For the Left, this was not enough. The Socialists, led by the leader of their left-wing, Francisco Largo Caballero, deserted the Popular Front and declared the need for immediate social revolution. The Anarchists denounced both Socialists and liberals and urged that the Republic give way to an Anarchist revolution. Azaña and his liberal cabinet felt helpless.

At the other end of the political spectrum, the Rightists had all but given up hope of peaceful reform through electoral victory. Like the extreme Left, the Right could achieve its goals only through violent rebellion. The Right was not, however, organized for subversion and scarcely knew what policy to follow. The Rightists were themselves repudiated by the small Spanish fascist movement, *Falange Española,* which preached a nationalist revolution to revitalize Spain and to benefit all social classes. The Falange, however, lacked the membership to be effective. The same can be said of the extreme reactionary wing of the monarchists (the Carlists), who had militia squads already training but whose support was limited mainly to the Pyrenean province of Navarre.

The only institution capable of effective reaction against the Popular Front was the army. By 1936 the officers had almost all come to regard the Republic as their enemy. They also hated the regionalist movements for destroying national unity, and they were determined to suppress subversion by the working class. The junior officers had, several years earlier, formed a conspiratorial association to plot overthrow of the Republic. Now, some of the leading generals began to work together for this end.

By late spring of 1936, public order in Spain had nearly disintegrated. Hundreds of strikes played havoc with economic life; gunmen from the various radical groups assassinated scores of people in the streets of the larger cities. Azaña, who had been raised to the figure-head position of the presidency, seemed totally unable to control the situation. In this environment, Spanish Communism began to thrive.

The Communist Party had numbered scarcely more than 1,000 members in 1931 and had played only a minor role in the abortive revolution of 1934. The radical scene of 1936 seemed perfectly suited to the Party's purposes. Funds from Russia had helped support the dependents of those arrested for complicity in the 1934 revolt; now a great deal of money was invested in propaganda and literature that flooded Spain. The Communists posed as the wave of the future, as the only proletarian movement that really understood revolution. They were actually playing a double game, for the official Party line was to support the moderate government of the Popular Front. The actual numerical following of the Communists was still small, and the Communists themselves understood, as did no other working-class party, the basic weakness of the Spanish Left.

During May and June, army plotters tried to draw the threads of conspiracy together. They were disgusted with all the politicians of Right and Left. They agreed among themselves that only the temporary control of a military regime could "save Spain." After several false starts, the military rebellion began in Morocco on July 17, 1936. Within forty-eight hours it spread to garrisons throughout the peninsula. The Republican government did not know where to turn for help. The Rightist parties supported the army, and the only alternative was the revolutionary movements—which wanted to overthrow the Republic for their own ends. The Socialists and Anar-chists demanded arms from the government so that they could oppose the military rebels. Reluctantly, feeling as though they had collectively slit their own throats, the Republican government distributed arms to the revolutionary workers' militia.

The military rebellion was poorly organized and the troops badly equipped. The Republican police and the sheer weight, as well as the suicidal bravery, of the revolutionary militia, snuffed out the rebellion in the major cities. However, in the far south and in the conservative provinces of the north and northwest, the army gained a foothold for what began quickly to look like a civil war.

The only efficient segment of the Spanish Army was composed of units stationed in Morocco. However, the revolt in the Navy failed, and the military leaders were unable to transport their troops to the mainland. The garrison troops in rebellion in the north badly lacked ammunition. During these first days, the rebel movement seemed on the verge of collapse.

From the foregoing, it is clear that the civil strife in Spain began as a domestic affair. Foreign agents, Communist or Nazi, had little to do with it. However, the army leaders—General Franco in Morocco and General Mola in the north —had quickly to seek assistance abroad to provide supplies and maneuverability for their forces. Very naturally, they turned to the fascist governments of Germany and Italy, governments which would presumably want to encourage an authoritarian nationalist regime in Spain. After some deliberation, Italy and Germany—independently and at first without knowledge of each other's actions—decided to send airplanes and military equipment to the Spanish rebels.

This help enabled General Franco to move his troops across to the peninsula in the latter part of the summer of 1936. Franco quickly organized a drive north toward Madrid and made rapid progress against the disorganized Loyalists (as the Republicans were often termed). The arming of the revolutionary militia in Madrid, Barcelona, and elsewhere temporarily deprived the constitutional authorities of control. They saw themselves swamped by Socialists and Anarchists who seized command of most aspects of political and economic life. (Largo Caballero, left-wing Socialist, became premier of the reorganized government.)

From the very beginning, outbreak of the civil war occasioned considerable alarm in other European capitals. The Spanish government soon claimed its right under international law to purchase military equipment in order to repress a seditious movement. The British and French, however, were reluctant to sell arms to the Republic. In the first place, they feared Leftist revolution in Spain. More importantly, they dreaded involvement in a civil war that might see Germany and Italy ranged on the other side, for such a situation could result in international conflict. Accordingly, the British and French tried to avoid any kind of involvement in the Spanish crisis. The western democracies hit on the idea of a "Non-Intervention" pact by which all nations would agree not to aid or intervene on either side in Spain. Twenty-six nations signed the agreement and sent representatives to sit in a special "Non-Intervention Committee" which endeavored to localize the struggle. With superb hypocrisy, Germany and Italy became members of the London Non-Intervention Committee. The French and British governments considered German and Italian aid to the rebels as the price paid to avoid world war. In parallel action, the United States embargoed shipments to Spain (January 8, 1937).

Other than Mexico—who could do little —the only nation to give substantial aid to the Republicans was the Soviet Union. The Soviet government was apprehensive over the spread of fascist power in central Europe and feared an authoritarian Rightist regime in Spain. Furthermore, the chaotic revolutionary situation in the Republican zone provided opportunities for the extension of Communist influence. And, if worst came to worst, Russian support to the Republic might be used as a pawn in the deadly diplomatic game played with the fascist states. For all these reasons, the Soviet Union attempted to strengthen the Republican resistance. The first Russian aid, along with a few military advisors, had been dispatched shortly after the fighting began. Then, in mid-September, military equipment was sent in large quantities. In addition, Communist authorities took the lead in organizing a special international military force, the famous "International Brigades," composed largely of Communist volunteers from the various nations of Europe. British, American, and Canadian volunteers formed the XVth International Brigade.

By the beginning of November, 1936, a rebel column, 20,000 strong, stood outside Madrid. To seize a city of one million with so small a force was no easy task, but the revolutionary militia had hitherto been able to offer so little resistance in the field that rebel leaders felt confident. Just at this time, however, Russian military aid began to arrive, and some of the militia units began to reveal traces of military cohesion. In an epic struggle, the columns of General Franco were stopped short in the suburbs of the capital. During the three months that followed, the rebels attempted to flank Madrid. As the military strength of the defenders increased, the flanking maneuvers failed.

By the first months of 1937, it had become clear that both sides had missed any opportunity to bring a quick end to the war. The military rebels controlled approximately 50 per cent of Spain's territory, mostly the western half of the country. In preparation for a prolonged struggle, the rebels had established a regular government on October 1, 1936. The Chief of State was General Franco, selected for the post of military dictator by several dozen companions. He commanded the most important segment of the rebel forces, had more prestige than any other general, was reputed to be politically shrewd, and was, therefore, a logical choice. The "National Movement," as the rebellion was now called, was entirely controlled by the army, and the army itself was, of course, directly under the orders of General Franco, the "Caudillo" or "Leader." The Nationalists' dictatorship was more than a military tyranny. It was also a dictatorship that relied on, and received, spiritual support from the Spanish Catholic Church. The clerical hierarchy eventually gave its official endorsement to the "Movement," not as a mere political or military enterprise but as a sacred Crusade against liberal and revolutionary influences in Spain.

On the other side of the barricades, discipline and order were slowly restored. During the first months of 1937, the Republican government began to recover authority which had been seized by the workers' militia. Coherent organization was achieved on the basis of a strange alliance between the Republican liberals, the right-wing Socialists, the bourgeois regional separatists and the Communists. From the very beginning, the Communists had eschewed efforts at social revolution and had worked for total concentration on military victory. In this they were diametrically opposed by the revolutionaries—the Anarchists, left-wing Socialists, and the small Trotskyist POUM organization in Catalonia. These revolutionaries wanted a social revolution—with or without the defeat of General Franco. In view of the precarious military situation, Communist policy made a great deal of sense, and the Communists helped the Republican government force the revolutionary elements into line.

Since the beginning of the war, Communist influence had increased greatly in Republican Spain. This was for two reasons: the Communists possessed the most unified and disciplined organization; and they had the prestige and support of the Soviet Union, which seemed the Republic's only friend and was the Republic's chief support. With these advantages, the Spanish Communist Party could not help but play a vital role in the politics of the Republic. Nonetheless, the Party did not at any time win the allegiance of the working class. The Party's tens of thousands of new adherents came rather from middle class and professional groups who saw in the Communists' discipline and strength their best hope for the future. Paradoxically, Spanish Communism was, in part, able to grow because it stressed order instead of revolution.

The independent power of the Anarchists and Trotskyites in the northeast (Catalonia) was broken after a brief rebellion in Barcelona (May 3–7, 1937). The would-be revolutionaries were defeated by the forces of the government (who were in large part led by the Communists). The Communists were completely under control of Moscow and had received orders to eliminate all signs of "Trotskyism" in the Republican zone. (Some authorities think that the Communists might even have made the first moves in this civil war within a civil war.) The Trotskyist leaders of the small POUM group were arrested and their leader tortured to death. The Anarchists were chastened by the suppression of their POUM allies.

During the first months of the civil war there had taken place perhaps as many as 75,000 murders of Rightists and others who happened to get in the way of revolutionaries in the Republican zone. These killings, which included the death of some 7,000 priests and nuns, had been carried out mainly by the Anarchists and left-wing Socialists. Irregular murders ceased, however, after the end of 1936. There was even liberty to re-open some of the Catholic churches, all of which had previously been closed.

The simple Catholic/anti-Catholic split which supposedly defined the Nationalist-Loyalist struggle was complicated by the fact that the Basque regionalists (or Basque "Nationalists") fought on the Republican side because the Republic had granted them regional autonomy soon after the struggle began. The Basques were among the most devout Catholics in Spain, but they had also become political liberals. The restoration of order by Communists and Republican liberals under premier Juan Negrín (who replaced Francisco Largo Caballero after the Barcelona troubles) was welcome to the Basques.

Throughout 1937, Communist influence increased on the Republican side. Because of the importance of Russian military aid, the Communists were able to control over half the military commands in the new Republican army. Russian generals served as ex-officio advisors and helped to plan Republican strategy. Special Red Army combat crews were brought to try out new Russian tanks and airplanes. Most sinister of all, a special section of the NKVD (the Soviet secret police) was introduced into Spain to eliminate anti-Communists and to maintain security. These forces, known as the "Checas," acted independently of the Republican government and set up secret prisons all their own in Madrid, Valencia, Barcelona, and elsewhere.

It would be a mistake, however, to assume from this that the Communists ever came to "control" the Republic. The prime minister for the last two years of the war, Juan Negrín, was by no means a Communist. But he did want to win the war, and he realized that the Communists provided the only source of supplies for embargoed Spain. Furthermore, he knew that the Communists were the only effective and organized political group on whom he could rely to concentrate on the war effort. For these reasons, Negrín chose to deal with the Communists. Nevertheless, with all their advantages, the Communists remained a minority party and never commanded more than three posts in the Republican cabinet. The cabinet was always dominated by a loose coalition of Republican liberals and right-wing Socialists.

The political problems of General Franco's government were much simpler. The Caudillo recognized that, in a civil war, some kind of civilian organization was needed to maintain popular support. Accordingly, in March, 1937, the Nationalist government took over the fascistic Falange organization and expanded it into a broad state-party for a new "totalitarian," yet Catholic, regime. There was no other party than the Falange, itself not so much a political party as an "instrument of national unification" containing a hodge-podge of all political forces under a bureaucratic state organization. Its vaguely fascistic ideology stressed authoritarianism unity, a corporative system of economic control, the revival of national energy and a more vigorous foreign policy. Fascists, Carlists, clericals, moderates, apolitical businessmen, ex-Anarchists—all were pressed into the new Falange, which represented everything and nothing. The important institution was the army, which provided discipline and leadership. No other party was permitted.

The army also bore responsibility for the fierce repression in the Nationalist zone. Before the rebellion, General Mola had written in secret instructions that the repression "must be violent in the extreme" in order to crush the radical Left before it could strike back. From the first day of the war, the military authorities implemented this directive. In the process, a distinct difference could be noted between the character of the political murders in the two zones. In the Republican zone almost all the slaughter occurred during the first six months. It had been spontaneous, unorganized, and against the desires of the Republican government. In the Nationalist zone, murder of the political opposition had from the very beginning been encouraged and organized by the official leadership. As the war went on, it grew rather than diminished in intensity, until the Nationalists had shot as many or more people than the Left revolutionaries.

Just as in the Republican zone, where the conflict had been greeted with wild joy by the lower classes, so in Nationalist Spain the beleaguered middle classes and the Catholic peasantry responded with intense enthusiasm. Threatened for five years by secularism and the prospect of social revolution, the peasants took up arms in defense of the traditional standards of Spanish society. Their dedication and courage was equal to that of the Leftists.

All the same, there was little doubt that the Republican cause was the more "popular" one. Perhaps as many as 40 per cent of the people supported the liberal and Leftist groups. The Rights' support came from a somewhat smaller group. However, what General Franco's government may have lacked in popular appeal it made up for in energy and discipline. In place of the confusion and insubordination that characterized the Republican army, Franco's forces were strictly disciplined. No less than 95 per cent of the regular officers in the former army served Franco. They provided the cadres to create an effective force.

Equally important, the Nationalists' German and Italian benefactors had determined to see Franco's government through the war. Every item in modern military equipment was shipped to the Nationalists. The Germans and Italians each supplied special air corps units. Mussolini pledged his own prestige to a Franco victory. Early in 1937, he sent a special Italian army corps of 30,000 men to fight with the Nationalists. The flow of reinforcements and supplies ceased only with the victory parade.

Stalin was never as eager to support the Republic as Hitler and Mussolini were to sustain General Franco. Russian aid moved only by fits and starts and, even at its maximum, was hardly so significant as the German and Italian shipments. Stalin's hesitation, together with the fact that the Republican army never developed into an efficient military machine, made Republican prospects look increasingly dim after the end of 1937. In the middle of that year, the Basque resistance had been crushed in the north.

The remaining Republican footholds in the northwest were progressively eliminated. Although Republican forces had beaten off Franco's assaults around Madrid and soundly defeated the Italians at Guadalajara, successive Republican efforts to seize the offensive achieved very limited gains.

During the winter of 1938, Franco's military preponderance mounted. All efforts by the Republican government to persuade the democracies to change their "Non-Intervention" policy failed. Conservative leaders in Britain and France seemed to welcome a Nationalist victory in Spain. The fact that Germany and Italy made Franco's success possible had ominous significance for the democracies. It was plain that a triumphant Nationalist dictatorship would be aligned with the fascist powers, but the western leaders were "too practical" to think ahead. Conservative and Catholic groups in Europe and America vociferously urged their governments to keep hands off, to allow General Franco to win, to avert the possibility of a Leftist revolution in Spain.

Within one month of the launching of a major offensive in March of 1938, the Nationalists had cut through to the Mediterranean coast and divided the Republic in half. By now the great enthusiasm of the lower classes of Madrid and Barcelona had dwindled toward defeatism. Hunger, privation, and military defeat took their toll, but Catholic, traditional Spain and modern, agnostic Spain were divided by rivers of blood; no easy termination of the war was yet in sight. The Republican forces rallied and stopped Franco's advance by mid-summer of 1938. In one of its most heroic efforts, the Republican army counter-attacked across Catalonia's Ebro River. The battle on that front lasted for most of the second half of 1938. When it was over, the totally exhausted Republicans had used up most of their best equipment. Franco's troops, thanks to Italy and Germany, were stronger than ever.

By the end of 1938, Stalin had decided to write off the Spanish venture and to terminate Russian aid to the Republic. A basic factor here was the September capitulation of the western democracies at Munich. If France and Britain would not resist the Nazi advance in central Europe, then Russia could not afford to support the Spanish Republic in the west. Such unaided support would merely weaken the Soviet Union and provide Hitler with further opportunities. As the fascist powers went on from victory to victory, Stalin decided to retrench, to shorten his lines, and to prepare for whatever might come.

In December of 1938, the situation of the Republic was hopeless. Negrín carried on desperately in the expectation that a general war would soon break out in Europe, a war which would force the democracies to come to the Republic's aid. Then, Franco's final offensive began. Within six weeks, Barcelona and all of Catalonia fell. The Republican zone was reduced to Madrid and the southeast quarter of Spain. Without aid from Russia, with the western democracies hastening to recognize Franco as the ruler of Spain, the end seemed only a matter of time.

Defeat deepened the rancor and rivalry which always existed inside the Republican camp. By February of 1939, some of the non-Communist officers in the Republican army were ready to surrender. They, together with many Socialist and Anarchist leaders, thought that further resistance was a useless spilling of blood. Furthermore, they increasingly resented the power and influence of the Communists and the unreliable and capricious nature of Russian aid. Infuriated by the sight of Russian secret police operating with impunity and by the spectacle of Communist officers in control of large sections of the Republican army, they demanded of Negrín that he make peace.

The prime minister replied that Franco's attitude made this impossible. Franco seemed vengeful and unrelenting, gave no guarantee of mercy to the vanquished, and demanded unconditional surrender. But, to the non-Communist officers of the Republic, Franco's harsh terms were better than a continuation of the hopeless struggle. The civil war ended as it had begun, with a revolt against the Republican government by its own army. Negrín was forced to flee, the Communist leaders did likewise, and the Communist military commanders were brought under non-Communist control. Then, at the end of March, 1939, the new commanders of the Republican zone surrendered to General Franco. The Spanish Civil War was over.

No other development "between the wars" had meant so much to so many people, throughout the western world, as did the Spanish war. Although it was primarily a struggle for control of Spain, fought by a myriad of Spanish factions, many saw it as a fight between religion and Red Revolution or as a struggle between fascism and democracy. In the light of three decades it is easier to see that the factions were many and the issues complicated; the cause of religion was compounded with outright murder and fascist dictatorship, and the cause of democracy was confounded with repression, assassination, and the threat of anarchy. The result was not so definitive nor the consequences so dire as partisans claimed at the time. The triumph of General Franco meant a quarter-century of Catholic authoritarianism in Spain. The problems of Spain remain unsolved —as strikes, repression, and the constant threat of renewed civil conflict attest.

II. THE EMBARGO CONTROVERSY

From The Nation: PRO-FASCIST NEUTRALITY

Founded by E. L. Godkin in 1865, the Nation *is one of the most important of the liberal weeklies. Its position on the Spanish Civil War was very strongly pro-Republican. When the editors heard of President Roosevelt's determination to seek an embargo against the Republic, they protested in an editorial which, ironically, appeared the day after the hastily adopted resolution was signed into law.*

A MAJOR sensation was created this past week by the "discovery" that the Neutrality Act had no bearing on the Spanish conflict. Although this fact was pointed out last August by the State Department itself, some of the sensational newspapers have sought to give the impression that the crafty Robert Cuse—alleged to be a Soviet agent because he once made sales to Russia—had ferreted out a "loophole" in the existing neutrality legislation and through it was planning to dispatch a lot of airplane parts to the Spanish government. The result has been a veritable clamor from the reactionary papers, supported, we regret to say, by Mr. Roosevelt himself, for a broadening of the act to include civil conflicts. Suggestions have also been made that all Americans who participate in the Spanish struggle be deprived of their citizenship, and that the law be strengthened to include raw materials and other potential war supplies.

To much in the argument of the neutrality advocates we can give unqualified support. We agree, of course, that America's commercial and financial relationships led it into the last war and are likely to lead it into the next one. We agree as to the necessity for adding raw materials and other war supplies to the list of articles to be embargoed in the event of war. We would give full support to Senator Vandenberg's contention that the rules of neutrality must be laid down in advance of a war because "the exercise of discretion after a war has started inevitably invites an unneutral interpretation by any belligerent which is curtailed or offended by the decision."

Unfortunately, neither the President nor Senator Vandenberg appears to have noted the pertinence to the Spanish situation of this last argument. Here is a war already in existence. Under international law American citizens are prohibited from aiding the military clique which has risen up against the duly elected government of Spain. In the past the United States has never challenged this law. On the contrary, we were insistent, at the time of our own Civil War, on the scrupulous observance of the rule; and have repeatedly hidden behind it when supporting puppet Latin American dictatorships of our own choosing. To take action now in denying supplies to the Spanish government in its hour of need would be a deliberately unfriendly act. It would be worse than merely to accord the rebels belligerent rights to

"Pro-Fascist Neutrality," *The Nation,* CXLIV (January 9, 1937), pp. 33–34.

which they are not entitled. With Hitler openly aiding the insurgents, a general embargo by the United States, like the European non-intervention agreement, would be denying the government the resources of which the rebels are actually availing themselves. An embargo against Spain and Germany would be as bad, since no munitions are normally shipped to the Reich. The United States would in effect be taking sides in the Spanish conflict, and taking the side of the Spanish militarists, Hitler, and Mussolini against the government chosen by the Spanish people. Nor could there be any pretext that Congress was merely enforcing a principle agreed upon in pre-war days. There was never any intention of applying the Neutrality Act to civil war. In acting in the midst of the battle, Congress is responding to the passions of the moment. And we need not look very far to find what interests in America are anxious for a fascist victory in Spain.

Much the same indictment can be made of the movement to enact neutrality legislation which would be mandatory in its application. We have already moved past the point where neutrality can be considered in terms of a hypothetical next war. The next war is upon us, and it is almost certain that it will be a war of aggression precipitated by Hitler with or without the aid of Mussolini. Ranged against the fascist powers will be France, the Soviet Union, and almost as surely England. It happens that England and France are much more dependent on supplies from the United States than Germany. Any announcement by the United States that it will not under any circumstances furnish the belligerent countries with the sinews of war is an open invitation to Hitler to launch his attack. Supplies that are denied the democratic countries would be just as useful to Hitler as the same amount of supplies sealed and delivered to Nazi Germany. Neutrality regulations which could be lifted in case the League found a certain country to be the innocent victim of aggression would not be open to this objection. If this country is to depart from traditional neutrality, let it at least be sure that it is not actively supporting fascism.

THE DEBATE IN CONGRESS ON THE EMBARGO OF JANUARY 8, 1937

The President's request for an embargo was presented to the Senate, on January 6, 1937, by Key Pittman of Nevada, Chairman of the Committee on Foreign Affairs. Almost simultaneously, Representative Samuel McReynolds of Tennessee, whose position corresponded to that of Pittman, took the resolution to the floor of the House. The debate was spirited. Behind the debate stood two facts of political life: the Nye Committee's exposure of "war-profits" during World War I (and the resultant conviction that we had been duped into war by munitions manufacturers and international bankers) and the President's overwhelming electoral triumph of November, 1936.

Senators and Representatives Participating in the Debates on Spain

SENATORS

Thomas T. Connally	Democrat, Texas
Gerald P. Nye	Republican, North Dakota
Key Pittman	Democrat, Nevada
Arthur H. Vandenberg	Republican, Michigan

REPRESENTATIVES

Thomas R. Amlie	Progressive, Wisconsin
John T. Bernard	Farmer-Laborite, Minnesota
Gerald J. Boileau	Progressive, Wisconsin
Hamilton Fish, Jr.	Republican, New York
James Hamilton Lewis	Democrat, Illinois
Maury Maverick	Democrat, Texas
Samuel D. McReynolds	Democrat, Tennessee
John E. Rankin	Democrat, Mississippi
Samuel Rayburn	Democrat, Texas
Harry Sauthoff	Progressive, Wisconsin

Senate

MR. PITTMAN. Mr. President, I am about to do something that is unusual, but that has heretofore been done. I present a joint resolution and ask unanimous consent for its immediate consideration without reference to a committee, and that it may be passed and signed without delay notwithstanding the rules. If the Senate will permit me, I shall make a brief statement of the nature of the joint resolution and then have it read.

The joint resolution simply makes it unlawful to export arms, ammunition, or implements of war from the United States

From the *Congressional Record* (January 6, 1937), pp. 73–79, 87–94.

or any of its possessions, or to export to a foreign country for transshipment to Spain, or for the use of either of the opposing parties in Spain during the present internal strife in that country.

MR. CONNALLY. Mr. President, will the Senator yield for a question.

MR. PITTMAN. I yield.

MR. CONNALLY. Does the joint resolution mention Spain, or just describe a condition that fits the situation in Spain?

MR. PITTMAN. It mentions Spain alone, and the reason for that determination, after consultation, to mention Spain alone was that we know exactly the conditions existing in Spain, and that such conditions of internal warfare necessitate an embargo on the export of arms, ammunition, and implements of war.

The question as to whether the term "civil war" applies or does not apply need not be determined. It would possibly be far more difficult to describe conditions generally that might arise in the future in a foreign country that would justify a similar embargo, and therefore we hesitated to make the resolution general. When I say "we," I refer to the President of the United States, to Representative McReynolds, to R. Walton Moore, Assistant and Acting Secretary of State, and to the legal branch of the Department of State.

As the Senator from Texas well understands, the Members of Congress have just arrived in Washington, and it has been impossible to get the committees together. It may be difficult to do so now.

I wish to have it distinctly understood, of course, that the joint resolution is mandatory; it is not a delegation of discretion or authority. It merely declares a certain thing to be unlawful so long as the strife referred to exists.

It goes further than that, however. The joint resolution makes it unlawful to export to any place for the use of either of the opposing forces in Spain any arms, ammunition, or implements of war produced in the United States. It so provides.

I readily understand, Mr. President, that there may be sympathy among our own citizens for one side or the other in the contest in Spain. Just as there is sympathy among some of the great governments and their nationals throughout the world for one side or the other in that great contest. I hope and believe that, so far as we are concerned, we are not, either mentally or physically or commercially, actively taking either side.

Let me remind those who have telegraphed to me suggesting that we are aiding the so-called insurgent government by this act that that is not a fact. The so-called insurgent forces in Spain control a tremendous portion of that country, if not the larger portion. They control a number of the ports. They have access to imports, just the same as the Government of Spain has, and, as a matter of fact, both forces are today receiving imports from countries whose governments or nationals are in sympathy with them.

There exists in Spain the most extraordinary condition of what may be called "civil war," if I may use that term, that has occurred in history, unless there was some parallel to it during the great Civil War in this country, and there certainly was not a complete parallel, because in Spain both forces are actually receiving arms, without blockade of their ports, from various powerful countries of the world. Both forces are being augmented by the soldiers of other powerful European countries. Not only that, but there is presented a situation which did not exist in our own Civil War, and which has not existed in any civil war I know of, where a great group of nations are threatening, without declaration of a state of war, to blockade all the ports of Spain, while some powers favorable to one side or the other are threatening to blockade only the ports controlled by the forces they oppose.

The facts with regard to this particular case are too well known to require debate. It is our duty, in my opinion, not to think of either of the opposing forces in Spain but to think of our own peace and our own country.

Two forms of government are fighting in Spain in what is called a "civil war," but it is a fight of foreign theories of government, not involving democracy, in which the opposing forces are aided and sympathized with by great, powerful governments who espouse one cause or the other.

Nothing would be gained by referring the joint resolution to the Committee on Foreign Relations. Our committee knows the facts with regard to the Spanish situation. Indeed, every Senator here knows the facts with regard to it.

The reason for presenting this matter as one of emergency is that our neutrality law has been held to apply only to a war between two foreign countries, and not to internal strife, not to a civil war. The legal branch of the State Department in honesty has so held, and two licenses have been granted to export airplanes and airplane parts to Spain. I do not know to which force they are going, nor am I aware that anyone else knows. It is known that the consignee is in Spain and he may be "John Doe." The granting of the first license was sufficiently disturbing but another application was made on yesterday, and, as a result

of the defect in our law, the license had to be granted, and over $4,000,000 worth of war materials, not alone airplanes but arms and ammunition and implements of war, have been authorized to be exported to parties in Spain. Whether those parties represent the insurgents or whether they represent the Government of Spain we cannot determine.

Mr. President, this practice should stop. There was a far less dangerous situation in 1914, which resulted in a World War into which we were dragged. An archduke was shot and killed in one of the countries of Europe. There was no great disturbance in that country and the great powers sought to arbitrate and compromise the difficulty. War broke out and swept the world and we were dragged into it, with a loss which can never be recovered. Today, say what we may, the situation is more dangerous than was the situation at that time. It is as dangerous as can be conceived. I say that it is our duty to pass this joint resolution at once, and I desire to present it at this time. . . .

THE VICE PRESIDENT. The joint resolution will be read.

The joint resolution (S.J.Res. 3) to prohibit the exportation of arms, ammunition, and implements of war from the United States to Spain, was read the first time by its title and the second time at length, as follows:

Whereas armed conflict of great magnitude is now and for several months has been carried on in the State of Spain, Continent of Europe, with all the weapons of war and of unusual brutality between the Government of Spain and a large and well-organized group of its nationals, commonly known as the insurgent forces; and

Whereas the Government of Spain and the so-called insurgent forces, each having possession of and asserting the legal and political control over parts of Spain and each attempting to prevent the opposition forces and the nationals claiming allegiance thereto from importing arms, ammunition, and implements of war; and

Whereas it is publicly asserted that some governments of Europe have recognized a so-called insurgent government and some governments are permitting their nationals to lend financial, commercial, and military aid to the so-called insurgent forces, while other governments are permitting their nationals to extend financial, commercial, and military aid to the Government of Spain; and

Whereas some of the principal governments of Europe have for a long time attempted to agree upon action that would prevent the shipment of arms, ammunition, and implements of war to either of the opposing forces in Spain and have sought to isolate Spain from foreign interference or intervention; and

Whereas said internal strife presents threats of extending beyond the borders of Spain and of involving other countries; and

Whereas the exportation from the United States of arms, ammunition, and implements of war to either of the opposing forces in Spain is dangerous to the security and peace of the United States and contrary to the policy of our Government as expressed by the President of noninterference in the internal affairs of a foreign state; and

Whereas an emergency exists requiring immediate legislative action: Therefore be it

Resolved, etc., That during the existence of the state of civil strife now obtaining in Spain it shall, from and after the approval of this resolution, be unlawful to export arms, ammunition, or implements of war from any place in the United States, or possessions of the United States, to Spain or to any other foreign country for transshipment to Spain or for use of either of the opposing forces in Spain. Arms, ammunition, or implements of war, the exportation of which is prohibited by this resolution, are those enumerated in the President's proclamation, no. 2163, of April 10, 1936.

Licenses heretofore issued under existing law for the exportation of arms, ammunition, or implements of war to Spain shall, as to all future exportations thereunder, *ipso facto* be deemed to be canceled.

Whoever in violation of any of the provisions of this resolution shall export, or attempt to export, or cause to be exported, either directly or indirectly, arms, ammunition, or implements of war from the United States or any of its possessions, shall be fined not more than $10,000 or imprisoned not more than 5 years, or both.

When in the judgment of the President the conditions described in this resolution have ceased to exist he shall proclaim such fact, and the provisions hereof shall thereupon cease to apply. . . .

MR. VANDENBERG. Mr. President, I wish to make a brief observation regarding the pending request of the able Senator from Nevada [Mr. Pittman] in respect to emergency neutrality action. Regardless of whether the initial offensive shipment out of New York into the troubled European area does or does not leave before we can reach it with corrective legislation, I think everyone will have to concede that there exists an imminent situation which requires immediate attention; and it is my entire disposition, so far as I am personally concerned, to cooperate in every possible way. I do this with less reluctance than would ordinarily attach to such summary action because the pending joint resolution is in no sense discretionary. It is mandatory.

We all want to reach the same objective, and the only problem is the method. But, Mr. President, I desire to associate myself definitely and specifically with the observations submitted by the able senior Senator from Missouri [Mr. Clark], who now occupies the chair, and who commented upon the problem confronting the Senate before the recess. I want to make it plain that from my point of view it would have been infinitely preferable and infinitely wiser and safer to have added to the existing neutrality statute the simple prohibitory language originally suggested by the Senator from Nevada [Mr. Pittman] himself, which would have met a general situation with a general remedy instead of inviting specific prejudices with a joint resolution aimed at one vicissitude alone.

However, since we seem to be beyond the deliberative point where that course can be followed if we are to meet the emergency, and since the only problem is the joint resolution pending, I wish to make one suggestion in connection with it to the able chairman of the committee. I should like to eliminate the preamble, because it deals with many contentious matters that are none of our business. It seems to me that the fewer words we use the better, because the fewer we shall then have to quarrel about or explain, or perhaps some day take back. The preamble is not necessary to the authority proposed to be conferred. I suggest to the able Senator that all the "whereases" are entirely unnecessary to the body of the joint resolution or to the validity of the action which we contemplate. On the other hand, the "whereases" contain numerous statements which might prove to be equivocal and embarrassing; and I want to ask the Senator, the chairman of the Foreign Relations Committee, if he is willing that the preamble be eliminated from the joint resolution. . . .

MR. PITTMAN. I wish to say, so that when the question is put there will be an understanding, that I have no objection whatever to the elimination of the "whereas" clauses. They were really placed in the joint resolution after very careful considerations—and I think they are true—for the purpose of inducement, and to show there is an emergency. There being no longer any such need, I am perfectly willing to have them stricken. I think it is better legislative practice to have the "whereas" clauses stricken from a measure before passage.

MR. VANDENBERG. Then, as I understand, Mr. President, the "whereases" are eliminated, and it is only the joint resolution which is pending, with request for consent for immediate consideration. On that basis I myself have no objection.

THE VICE PRESIDENT. Is there objection to the request of the Senator from Nevada for unanimous consent for the present consideration of the joint resolution?

MR. NYE. Mr. President, reserving the right to object, I wish to say that there seems to be quite general and united opinion that the peace of the United States is threatened by reason of certain contracts which have been entered into calling for delivery of American supplies to Spain. I do not for one moment desire to take a different attitude upon that point. I do think that our peace is in some degree jeopardized—not so greatly as many would have us believe—but when our peace is jeopardized I think we, as Members of the Congress, should assume the right to take whatever steps are necessary, however drastic or however unfair they may seem to be at the moment.

I am not entertaining a sympathy with either side represented in the conflict which is raging in Spain at the moment. We have a policy of government respecting neutrality. Our policy of neutrality, rather hurriedly adopted during the past 2 years, has not covered the situation which has arisen in Spain, but our Government has sought cooperation on the part of Americans in a program that was intended to avoid the very embarrassment which is upon our doorstep at this time.

I think it ought to be said to the everlasting credit of those who are recognized as the leaders in the United States in the business of manufacturing and selling munitions of war that they have cooperated with the Government. I think it fair that we should pay them a tribute at this hour in appreciation of the manner in which they have cooperated with the Government. After making inquiries concerning the policy of the Government respecting shipments of arms to Spain, the leaders in that particular business have declined to deal with Spain. It had begun to appear that even without a definite written policy governing situations of the kind we are now considering we should have avoided embarrassment except for the fact that an individual American junk dealer, making inquiry of our Government as to its policy, or knowing what the policy was, willed to ignore that policy, came and laid his fee for license upon the desk of the State Department, and demanded license to ship arms to the Spanish Government. It seems to me that that action warrants our pursuing now a course which but for such action would be altogether unfair—indeed, unreasonable.

However, in that connection I should like to point out that although our embarrassment was directly occasioned by this lone American dealer in second-hand munitions of war, the supplies with which that dealer is involved at the present moment are the cast-offs of our own American Military Establishment, sold at public auction to this type of American, who has no respect for the policy of the Government; who has said, in effect,

"The policy of the Government be damned."

I should like to make the point that if the United States would nationalize the munitions industry, and if the United States would adopt a hard-and-fast policy of control over the part of the industry that was not nationalized, we should be able to avoid experiences of the present kind, and many more that are bound to arise to plague us.

I think it altogether fair to speak of the spirit in which we as a Government are moving at this time in calling for this embargo against the shipment of arms to Spain. That spirit—and I think I shall not be contradicted in so contending—is one which finds us desiring to cooperate with certain powers in Europe who conceive that they can hasten the end of the difficulty in Spain by denying arms to either side engaged in that conflict. In that spirit we have been advised that we could be helpful in avoiding a world war, or a war of great consequence, if only we would cooperate, and deny from our shores supplies of munitions to either side engaged there in Spain.

Now, however, the question arises as to other matters. We now are about to cooperate, to lend our support to that cause, to lay down a hard-and-fast rule that there shall be no exportation of munitions of war from the United States to Spain, or to either side engaged in war in Spain. We are going to cooperate with Great Britain and with France in what I conceive to be a splendidly conceived program of preventing a spread of the difficulty now confined within the borders of Spain. But what are we going to do if next week, or the following week, Great Britain and France make up their minds that since other powers in Europe are arming one side in Spain, it is only fair to arm the other side, and there is a chance of our expediting and speeding the end of the difficulty there by selling arms to the loyalist forces in Spain? . . .

Mr. President, unfair it will be to charge us with favoritism, because I believe there is no desire in a single mind in the Senate or in the House to favor any side in this present controversy. What we are trying to do is to save ourselves from the possibility of being drawn into a war. I do not believe there is a thought on the part of anyone that we want to help the Fascist element or that we want to help the Loyalist element. Certainly that is far from our thoughts.

But, in the light of our past contact with this question, why is it not going to be quite natural for the Fascist supporters the world over to say, "A year ago, when the interests of the Fascist elements in Italy were involved, the United States refused to take any hand in writing an embargo on oil because to have written it then would have constituted an unneutral act; but now they are aiding the cause of the Fascists in Spain by providing an embargo which is intended to meet the immediate contracts entered into by the Loyalist elements of Spain, with individuals in the United States to supply them with arms"?

Mr. President, if this action this afternoon is to be conceived, as I am going to conceive it, in the light of an effort to keep the hands of the United States clean and removed from the danger of being drawn quickly into that war or strife in Europe, I am quite willing that it shall be done; but I hope it is not going to be done in the name of neutrality, for, strictly speaking, neutrality it is not. . . . [*After further debate of several minutes, the Resolution passed, 81–0.*]

House

[Mr. McReynolds introduced the Senate's resolution and asked unanimous consent for suspension of rules and immediate passage.]

MR. MAVERICK. Mr. Speaker, I think this legislation is hasty and ill-advised. It was hasty and ill-advised last year, and there is no occasion for this sudden action. Why have we not been more fully advised? It just covers Spain. Why should we not apply it equally to all countries? The revolution in Spain has been going on for 7 months. It has always been the practice of our Government to send munitions to the legal government, irrespective of its merits. If we are to send munitions at all, send them to every nation—to Hitler or Mussolini, if they have a revolution. It has always been the policy of this Nation to maintain the *status quo* of the recognized parliamentary government or of the *de facto*, or even the Fascist government. Why, then, should we pick out Spain and suddenly say that we will pass this bit of emergency legislation? One of the criticisms of our Government has been that it indulges in hasty and ill-advised legislation. They have been killing each other over there in Spain for several months. What we do in the next few minutes will not amount to much; possibly they will kill each other for 10 hours more. We treated the American troops in that way around the time of the armistice. I want the gentleman to say why we should violate the precedents of 150 years, pick out Spain, and not pass a general law. I favor an embargo against every nation. . . .

[Mr. McReynolds] said when this comes up on the floor later he is willing for an amendment to be added which will make it apply to all countries. I am willing for it to apply to all countries now. Is the gentleman not willing to let this be considered for amendment, so that we can apply it to the British Empire and the German Fascist Government, and every other country? I say this because I hope we stop arms shipments to every country.

MR. McREYNOLDS. May I say to the gentleman there is no country where this could apply soon? This is an emergency, and for that reason we are asking that it apply only to Spain.

Within the next 2 or 3 weeks a general neutrality bill will be presented to the House in which there will be provision applying to civil war in any country and giving the President power to stop the shipment of armaments to those countries. . . .

Mr. Speaker, I ask the consideration of the membership and hope they will not insist on more than half an hour a side, for [this present] resolution is to be considered under the 5-minute rule. I hope no objection will be made. . . .

THE SPEAKER. The gentleman from Tennessee asks unanimous consent that this resolution may be considered in the House as in the Committee of the Whole, that general debate be limited to 1 hour, one-half to be controlled by the gentleman from Tennessee [Mr. McReynolds] and one-half by the gentleman from New York [Mr. Fish], at the expiration of which time the bill is to be read under the 5-minute rule.

Is there objection? [After a pause] The Chair hears none, and it is so ordered.

MR. BERNARD. Mr. Speaker, I object.

MR. BOILEAU. Mr. Speaker, a point of order.

THE SPEAKER. The gentleman will state the point of order.

MR. BOILEAU. I may state that the gentleman from Minnesota [Mr. Bernard] was on his feet and tried two or three times to gain the attention of the Speaker and to object. I am sure the Speaker did not see the gentleman from Minnesota, but he was on his feet attempting to make his objection. I therefore request the Speaker to give further consideration to the gentleman's wishes in this respect.

MR. McREYNOLDS. I think the gentleman's objection came too late.

MR. BERNARD. Mr. Speaker, I objected four times.

MR. McREYNOLDS. I understood the Chair had already ruled.

THE SPEAKER. Does the gentleman from Minnesota [Mr. Bernard] state to the Chair that he was on his feet objecting to the unanimous-consent request?

MR. BERNARD. Mr. Speaker, I objected four times.

THE SPEAKER. Was the gentleman on his feet when the Chair put the unanimous-consent request?

MR. BERNARD. I objected; yes.

THE SPEAKER. Objection is heard to the unanimous-consent request. . . .

MR. MAVERICK. Mr. Speaker, we are committing an act which is unneutral against the duly elected parliamentary Government of Spain, a parliamentary government like this Government, though we may not agree with it. There are two alternatives, at least there are in my mind. I am opposed to the shipment of munitions to any foreign country at all. I do not want to ship them to Spain and I do not want to ship them to Germany, but if Germany should have a revolution, she is entitled to the munitions as much as Spain. England is entitled to have them shipped. We are not being fair in this way in our international relations. To settle the question send no munitions out to any nation.

I am going to offer an amendment to make this apply to the whole world and I hope we will not waste any time in agreeing to it. Gentlemen say that they are going to bring in general neutrality laws in a short time. Do it now. Why wait? Let us have neutrality now and be fair to the whole world. [Applause]

MR. SAUTHOFF. Mr. Speaker, those of us who have fought consistently for neutrality in the last 2 years can at least feel that we are making some progress, although it has been slow, uphill work. I recall only too well last year when the Neutrality Act of 1935 was about to expire on the 29th day of February. Many of us could not get the bill then pending out of the present committee in order that we might have adequate time to debate it and offer amendments. When it finally did come out, after a group of us called upon the President and insisted that it be brought out, it was brought out under suspension of the rules, which prohibited amendment.

Had we been permitted to discuss this all-important subject fully and freely, instead of 40 minutes, as was the case, and had we been permitted to offer amendments at that time, we could have prevented, not only this situation but others that no doubt will arise because of inadequacy of discussion. Open discussion never injured any worthy cause, and neutrality is a most worthy cause.

The resolution refers only to civil war in Spain. Why not in other countries? Surely we are not going to make exceptions and thereby play favorites. Civil war may break out today, tomorrow—who knows when?—in some other country on this earth. Conditions are ripe in certain countries for just such a contingency. Why should we wait until it happens before we lay down a course of conduct? Is it because there are secret agreements

or unofficial assurances to favored nations as to what our conduct shall be? I, for one, wish to adhere to a sound policy of minding our own business. Therefore, I shall support [an amendment by which] all countries may be included in the scope of this measure. Personally, I favor a declaration which will declare it to be our national policy to prohibit shipments of munitions to any place any time when war, civil or otherwise, takes place.

I do not want to hurt anyone's sensitive feelings in this matter, but it is the fault of the committee that we are in our present predicament and that the Government of this country finds itself unable to act, because of the blunder that was made by the committee bringing it in under suspension of the rules, prohibiting us from placing any amendments on it. Now that blunder is to be repeated by this type of hasty, ill-considered, ill-advised legislation. We are being told that this resolution is to be offered because an emergency exists. There have been broadcasts in the newspapers of this country for the last 2 weeks telling about the sales of these munitions. Why was not a rule brought in yesterday? We were here. We had nothing else to do. We adjourned early. Why did we not debate the rule for a couple of hours on yesterday? Why were we not advised as to what this resolution was to be, and an opportunity given to have it printed, so that we might read it and consider amendments? We are forced to debate this subject without any copies of this resolution.

It seems to me that every time the subject of neutrality comes up we are faced with this same proposition that we have to fight every inch of the way to get the smallest and the least consideration to have full and open discussion. If we are all in favor of neutrality—and we claim we are—then why do we not have some neutrality, instead of talking about discouraging debate and harassing those who want to discuss it freely, and only too often come in with the suggestion that we proceed to its consideration without amendment?

The chairman of the committee suggests we will not have any such civil condition arising in any of the other countries and that we should pass this at once as an emergency measure. Much as I esteem the judgment of the chairman of the committee, I claim that he has no divine authority nor omniscient powers to judge whether or not there is going to be a civil war in any other country as well as in Spain. [Applause] . . .

MR. McREYNOLDS. I am very sorry we did not have the counsel of [Mr. Sauthoff's] wisdom and advice when we were trying to draw a neutrality bill at the last session. If he ever came before that committee or offered a suggestion, no one knows it, and no one knows yet that he had anything to do with bringing out the bill. What he seems to be mad about now is that last session when I brought the bill here, it could not be amended, and now he is mad because I have brought one here that can be amended. [Laughter and applause] That is his consistency.

I want to say to the distinguished gentleman that we reported out a bill, and I applied to the Rules Committee for a rule, but later it was found that it could not be passed in the Senate. Then we compromised on the bill that was passed.

Are you neutral? Do you want neutrality? I want to save this country from becoming involved in European wars, and I shall not be a party to the carnage and crucifixion that is going on in Spain, and I want to see the eyes of the men in the House who will. That is the way I feel about it. [Applause]. . . . [Mr. Con-

nery of Massachusetts proposed an amendment by which the resolution would cover all nations.]

MR. AMLIE. As the resolution stands at the present time it is an unneutral act. It constitutes an unfriendly act toward a government that is friendly to the United States. Not long ago a newspaperman wrote that the significant thing about this strife in Spain was the fact that all of the world was taking sides in that contest. This is particularly true of the governments of European countries and of the classes in European countries. It is true, of course, of individuals as well.

It seems to me that at this time we ought not to take sides but ought, rather, to adopt a well-defined and adequate neutrality policy. I have been struck the last few weeks by the fact that Members of this body and Members of another legislative body, who have not distinguished themselves by their efforts in behalf of neutrality legislation, have been quoted by the press as to what they would do to prevent shipments of arms from this country to the regularly constituted Government of Spain. These people are not interested in maintaining the neutrality of the United States. These people are pro-Fascist, and they would like to have the United States take a stand that would help the Rebel-Fascist forces of Spain.

As far as I am concerned, I believe that George Washington, in his Farewell Address, enunciated a foreign policy for the United States that we would do well to follow. If we adopt the amendment of the gentleman from Massachusetts this resolution will then constitute an adequate and far-reaching statement of foreign policy applicable in all cases, and not open to the charge that it is designed to injure a friendly nation. [Applause]

[Here the gavel fell] . . .

MR. FISH. Mr. Speaker, there is no disposition on the part of the Republican minority to delay, obstruct, or hamper the majority in the passage of this bill. We recognize that this is an emergency measure, that it has for its purpose the preservation of peace, and keeping the United States out of war by preventing the selling of munitions and implements of war to either side in the civil war in Spain.

We as a minority regret that it is necessary for the House of Representatives to rush through legislation of this importance without adequate debate. It so happens that in the other body they struck out the entire preamble. Some of the Members of the House, including myself, spoke to a number of the Senators when the Senators were here a few hours ago at the joint session and suggested that this be done. It might well have happened that we would have passed the resolution containing the preamble. The preamble practically recognizes a state of belligerency by the Congress in Spain, yet our State Department has failed to issue any proclamation of belligerency or insurgency. The adoption of the preamble by Congress would have virtually declared a state of belligerency to exist in Spain, instead of such proclamation coming from the President or from the State Department, and would have established an unfortunate precedent for future administrations absolutely contrary to international custom and tradition.

I am in sympathy with the purposes of this joint resolution. As I previously stated, I regret there is not adequate debate provided to discuss the bill intelligently and the present conditions in Spain. The resolution amounts to a complete change of the policy of the United States. If I am wrong in the statement I am about to make, I wish some Member would correct me.

As I recollect it, the Congress some years ago authorized the Chief Executive to permit the shipment of arms to *de facto* governments in South and Central America. In other words, we prohibited the shipment of arms to the insurgents or to the rebels against the existing governments in Central and South America.

We are now making a complete about-face in this resolution as far as Spain is concerned, which is the *de facto* or recognized government, as we have failed to recognize the insurgents, and provide that the Spanish Government shall not be allowed to buy arms and munitions of war in the United States. However, I favor the policy outlined in this bill because I think it is a step in the direction of peace and that we should not sell arms or munitions of war to either side. . . .

This is an emergency measure, and we on our side do not propose to play politics with it for partisan reasons. I am sure that most of the Republican Members will support the bill in its present form, or as amended, in order to stop the sale of American munitions to both sides in Spain, for the sake of war profits and blood money.

I think the gentleman from Texas made the statement that this bill goes farther than the wording of the bill indicates. It is not merely a question of stopping the shipment of arms and munitions of war to the different factions in Spain. The whole world at the present time is filled with rumors of war and is on the verge of a world war that may start in Spain at any moment.

We have to determine our neutrality policy. We have to determine now whether we will sacrifice war profits and blood money in order to keep out of these wars. I think that is the desire and will of the American people at this time. You can almost hear the beating of the wings of the Angel of Death as it hovers over Spain tonight or France, Germany, China,

Japan, or Soviet Russia. We peace-loving Americans have to determine whether we will sacrifice the war profits that dragged us into the last war by adopting a strict, permanent neutrality policy prohibiting the sale and shipment of arms and munitions of war to all belligerent countries. As one who served in the World War and as one who loathes and abhors wars, I am in favor of stopping the sale of munitions of war to all belligerent nations and civil-war factions within a nation. . . .

MR. RANKIN. Mr. Speaker, as a great American once said, "It is a condition and not a theory that confronts us."

In my opinion we should pass this resolution as written, at the earliest possible moment, and by a roll-call vote, in order to let the American people and the world know just how strongly the Congress of the United States favors keeping us out of a foreign war. I agree that this policy ought to be carried further to apply to the entire world and I am willing to support legislation to that end at any time.

I agree with the gentleman [Mr. Fish] who stated a few moments ago that there ought not to be any more private enterprises manufacturing munitions of war. I have felt that for years, because I believe the munitions manufacturers and the international financiers have done more to drag us into war than everything else put together.

Let me say to the gentleman from New York [Mr. Fish], who talks about reversing the policy of 150 years, that I do not care if we are reversing the policy of a thousand years if it will keep us out of the holocaust of war now going on in Spain. The people of the world are not thinking technicalities. But when they look across the sea and behold helpless women and children ruthlessly killed with poison gases in the streets of Madrid or blown to pieces in the Alcazar [of Toledo], they shudder with horror. Our people expect us to keep them out of such a conflict. Remember, this is the way we started getting into the World War, through these munitions manufacturers and other people who were willing to endanger the peace of our country in order to coin their millions from the blood and tears of the suffering men, women, and children of the world. . . .

The gentleman talks about what we [Democrats] have done about taking the profits out of the next war. We have been trying to tax the profits of the last war. If his party had started in at the time the war closed, or when they took control of the Government in 1921, on a policy of taxing the profits made out of the last war, and made those who got rich out of it understand that wars were not to get rich from, you could not only have balanced the Budget and paid a large part of the national debt, but you would have served notice on these greedy munitions manufacturers and financiers that they were not going to sacrifice the American people in foreign wars in order to make for themselves millions or billions of paltry dollars at the sacrifice of millions of human lives in the years to come.

I sincerely trust that this measure will pass without amendment. We can amend later. This is an emergency. I also hope that we may have a roll call on its final passage.

Let us register our voices now so that the 130,000,000 people back home may understand that we are going to keep them out of any foreign wars, if it is humanly possible to do so. [Applause] *[After several minutes further debate, the Resolution passed, 411–1. 22 Representatives abstained from voting. Mr. Bernard was the only Representative to vote "Nay."]*

DEBATE IN CONGRESS ON THE NEUTRALITY ACT OF MAY 1, 1937

The embargo of January 8, 1937, was acknowledged to be an emergency measure. The Neutrality Act of 1935 was to expire May 1, 1937. Anxious to provide an improved version of neutrality legislation, Congress debated the "Pittman Resolution" (as the Neutrality Act of 1937 was known before its passage). The Resolution gave the President power to prohibit shipment of "arms, ammunition, or implements of war from any place in the United States" to any belligerent state or to any state involved in a civil war. The President was also given power to prohibit the export of any other "articles or materials" which might be destined for belligerent nations or factions, to halt the purchase, sale, or exchange of "bonds, securities, or other obligations of the government of any belligerent state or of any state wherein civil strife" existed, to prohibit American ships from carrying arms to belligerent states or factions, to prohibit Americans from traveling on the ships of belligerent states or factions, and to prohibit American ships engaged in trade with such states or factions from carrying any armaments other than small arms (for the protection of the ship itself).

The debate was mostly over the freedom of humanitarian groups to operate in belligerent nations and in nations torn by civil strife (which was allowed with little protest) and over the degree of discretionary power to be granted the President. This latter question brought forth the longest and most intense debates. The excerpt is from the last day of the prolonged consideration.

MR. VANDENBERG. Mr. President, I desire to speak very briefly on the conference report.

As the neutrality resolution passed the Senate, it seemed to me it went to the extreme border of Executive discretion which could be tolerated. As it comes back from the conference [with the House] so far as I am concerned it has crossed the limits of toleration in that respect.

It seems to me, Mr. President, that the neutrality resolution—in the form in which we now confront it—transfers a substantial portion of the war-making power from the Congress to the Chief Executive. Without the slightest thought of reflecting upon the wisdom or the patriotism or the peace-mindedness of any President, present or future, I am bound to assert my belief that this is a long step in the wrong direction. The most significant and controlling of all war decisions are not those that are made in the ultimate, formal act of a declaration of war. The most significant and controlling decisions, so far as our relationships to other people's wars are concerned, are the preliminary decisions which mold our initial attitudes toward other people's wars. The

From the *Congressional Record* (April 29, 1937), pp. 3943–44.

kind of neutrality we institute may well be the controlling factor in determining our ultimate destiny and our ultimate involvement in war itself.

To a considerable extent this was true in 1914–17. It is still more true today. In other words, the real war decision, so far as we are concerned, is actually made when we choose our neutrality formula. Under this resolution, Congress still keeps its constitutional right and responsibility to declare war, but as the conference report is written, Congress delegates controlling responsibilities over neutrality to the Chief Executive. Therefore, in whatever degree the neutrality decision is a war decision, this report invites us to declare war by Executive decree.

Mr. President, I am opposed to declarations of war directly or indirectly by Executive decree in a democracy. The field of exportable commodities, other than arms, ammunition, and implements of war, which are now transferred from the mandatory to the discretionary zone as the result of the Senate yielding to the House upon this proposition, touches the field of greatest controversy and the field of greatest friction; yet in this field the decision now goes to the White House and leaves the Congress behind.

Mr. President, it is my conviction—and I must state it again—that the only safe and practical neutrality rules are those which are written in advance of the necessity for their application. If neutrality decisions are postponed to the fatal hour when their application is immediately required, they will inevitably be construed in the light of their effect upon the immediate situation to which they attach. This promptly precipitates two unavoidable hazards:

First, no matter how impartial the decision may be intended by us to be, it is bound in physical fact to hurt one belligerent more than the other, and the belligerent which gets the worst of it will consider the decision to be unneutral, and the trail of resentment, if not of reprisal, starts.

Second, no matter how courageous a President may be in his purpose to reject selfish commercial considerations in established neutrality quarantines for us against other people's wars, if his neutrality decisions are discretionary, and if they are not made until wars are under way, it will be next to impossible for him to interrupt a profitable war commerce when once it has started. That comment applies specifically to the conference report as it now relates to our exportable business in commodities other than arms, ammunition, and implements of war.

If our neutrality formula is mandatory —so far as humanly possible to foresee the needs—and if it is written in advance of the need for its application, it can deal with the subject objectively. It can be free, on the one hand, from the prejudicial involvements which arise under the first hazard to which I have referred. It can be free, on the other hand, from the commercial influences which arise under the second hazard to which I have referred. But it can be free in no other way. It can be objective in no other way. It can be neutral in no other way. It can be pacific in no other way. It is precisely like the rules in any other game. They cannot be written or changed after the game begins if they are to preserve an atmosphere of accepted fair play and impartiality.

Therefore, as a fundamental proposition, still believing in the impossibility of a wide, large delegation of congressional authority to the Executive in respect to these decisions, and still feeling that the important thing is to establish the rules of the game in advance, so that all the world is upon notice in respect to them before the necessity for their application arises, I find myself keenly disappointed by the conference report.

I desire to say in that connection, however, that I think the joint resolution as it stands, on the basis of the conference report, produces many superbly progressive advancements in respect to war quarantine and isolation; but inasmuch as there is, in spite of this May 1 deadline, no pressing need for action, inasmuch as there is no immediate crisis breaking upon the horizon, and inasmuch as we might well, at least, take as much longer to consider the matter as it will take the President to return to Washington, it seems to me that the conference report might well be rejected and another effort made to bring the measure back at least a little closer to the theory upon which the Senate originally passed it. . . .

MR. LEWIS. The able Senator from Michigan [Mr. Vandenberg] makes a point that is generally indulged throughout the country, that something should be expressed prior to any difficulties in which the country may find itself, so that all may understand the position our country occupies on policies of neutrality. Such is oftentimes asserted by very eminent sources. . . .

But, sir, I make the point, in justification of my own position, that I feel in dealing with a foreign country in cases where the question arises as to what shall be done from time to time it is necessary to determine it on the basis of what the foreign country is doing from time to time, and there can be only one source which we can trust wholly, because of the system under which we operate under our laws and theory of government. That source is to the Commander in Chief of our forces of defense.

Mr. President, this country is not neutral. It is well for us to speak of our neutrality and it is a pleasing poetic sentiment. In the olden days the theory of neutrality was that we were neither one thing nor the other; that we were "hands off"; but in the present day, sir, this country cannot be neutral in feeling. If there is a controversy in foreign lands which involves human liberty and natural justice and natural rights as between mankind, essentially the United States at once becomes interested. Far from being neutral, she becomes essentially active in mind and thought and takes her position in sympathy with one or the other. All that can be done is that we restrain ourselves from action carrying out, if you please, sir, or executing our feelings upon the subject. Next, and more important, is that we do not disguise to the public our feelings. Furthermore, sir, we must cease being neutral as against the rights of America. In this respect we have been neutral too long. We seem to have remained neutral as to the rights of our own country but active in preserving the rights or claims of other countries. We too often have been perfectly neutral regardless of the effect on the United States of giving up its rights before the world. . . .

Mr. President, I respectfully insist, as I previously have asserted on this floor, that we cannot now put into any law specific declarations of what we will do under each arising circumstance, as we cannot tell until the circumstance arises what action it would call for—that the attitude of this Nation be left in the charge and discretion of those to whom there has been committed such control. I would, therefore, while conflicts are on between other nations of the world, place the privilege in the hands of the President to assert by regulation the course of conduct of the United States from time to time as conditions in other lands and the essential protection of ourselves may require. . . .

I ask my able friends if they do not realize that if the President should exercise the discretion, working a result that some of us fear or feel is possible, and his action did not meet with our approval, if Congress were in session it could promptly have a supervision of the whole subject and repeal the action of the President—veto, overthrow it—and at once, sir, it would become ineffective. If the Congress were not in session, and the President should exercise obnoxious privileges, an expression on the part of the representatives of the people of the country could be had, at once making known our viewpoint. It cannot be conceived that any President or any political party in America would assume, sir, to go counter to the interest of his own country for the gratification of a venal desire to bring about a declaration of war and the destruction of mankind; it cannot be assumed that the President of the United States, in his natural anxiety to preserve peace and to hold for his own people their privileges of liberty and justice, would take any other course by his regulation than that which is to benefit his country. . . .

[The bill, after extended discussion, passed by a vote of 41–15, with 39 abstentions. The bill passed the House after less extended debate (and without a role-call vote) and was signed by the President on May 1, 1937. On the same day, the President invoked the provisions of the Neutrality Act to maintain the embargo on Spain.]

Alfred M. Bingham: WARMONGERING ON THE LEFT

Public opinion was strongly divided on the wisdom of the embargo. Clergymen, doctors, educators, lawyers, and other groups formed committees and signed petitions to urge repeal or maintenance of the embargo. The most dramatic protests against the embargo came at the American Writers Congress of 1937. Newton Arvin, Van Wyck Brooks, Erskine Caldwell, Malcolm Cowley, Archibald MacLeish, Lewis Mumford, Clifford Odets, Upton Sinclair, Carl Van Doren, and several other writers sent out a call in which they argued that "Spain is the first real battlefield in a civil and international conflict that is certain to recur elsewhere. If the fascists are allowed to win in Spain, then France or Czechoslovakia or the Soviet Union is likely to suffer the next attack. It is hard to see how the United States can keep out of war once it begins on a world scale." At the Congress, which was held in New York, June 4–6, 1937, Archibald MacLeish, Ernest Hemingway, and a number of others urged American aid to Spain. At the very least, writers wanted an end to the embargo.

Protests of this sort, editorials in radical magazines and in liberal weeklies, petitions—these stirred Alfred Bingham to a different kind of protest. Bingham was a founder of the radical magazine Common Sense. *In* Common Sense, *Bingham, John Dos Passos, Theodore Dreiser, and others advocated American neutrality. They argued that the American Writers Congress did not truly represent American writers and that American Marxists imperiled hopes for the reformation of society by managers and technicians. During the summer of 1937, Bingham wrote a series of articles—including the one reprinted below—in which he followed this line and attacked "warmongering on the Left."*

THE bombing of the *Deutschland* [by the Loyalists] and the shelling of Almeria [by the German navy] in reprisal last month was one of the "international incidents" which makes the whole world hold its breath. Was this The War after all?

Because no nation wants to precipitate a general war—at least not yet—the "incident" evaporated. But in the first truculent movements, when the Fascist powers withdrew from the "Non-Intervention" Committee, and Mussolini announced that his navy would prevent Russian ships from reaching Spain, it was clear how near to war Europe was because of the Spanish situation. In the next similar incident, even though the direct will to war may still be absent, Mussolini's battleships may sink Soviet or French vessels, and the fuse may disappear in the powder.

It has already been suggested in these articles that if and when a general Euro-

From Alfred Bingham, "War Mongering on the Left," *Common Sense*, VI (July 1937), pp. 11–15.

pean war breaks out it will *not* be a war in defense of Democracy against Fascism. It will be made to appear so, however. Even the imperialists of Great Britain and France, whose contacts in this country will (as in 1917) be the determining influence in embroiling us, will join the labor and Marxist groups in their own countries to assail the "rape of Spain by the Fascist Huns." As the varied pressures, war orders, propaganda, financial commitments—are brought to bear against our neutrality, America will inevitably be drawn in. Our young men will once more go out to die for democracy—the democracy of the Soviet dictatorship, and British India, the democracy of French Indo-China and the Bank of England. And America will surely be drawn in, unless—

Unless American liberal thought and American Progressive politics are able to marshal all their strength against the warmakers. Unless they are able to apply all they have learned about the shams of 1917, about the futility and insanity of war, about the irrelevance of biased atrocity stories. Unless they are able to keep searching for the truth and sowing it in fertile ground.

And what is the truth behind the apparent confusion in the world today? For one thing, capitalism is giving way to collectivism, and in the process, as when feudalism gave way to capitalism, deep convulsions take place. Wars and revolutions are the penalty for the failure of intelligence to cope with the issues as they arise. Passions replace intelligence and bring forth violence, and, once violence is the rule, honest intelligence is almost impossible to regain.

At present many of those Americans who should be bravely insisting on tolerance and intellectual integrity are a prey to hysteria and dishonest thinking. Radicals who should be concentrating on the task of building Socialism are raising the slogan of a democracy which they do not believe in when applied to their own revolution. Liberals, who should be concerned with the fact that the majority of their fellow-Americans in this country are denied the right to live decently, indulge in orgies of indignation and tearful sympathy for the orphans of Guernica. (The starving Armenians, victims of Turkish atrocities, provided the escape once before.) The progressives, whose whole determination should be the discovery of means to a peaceful transition to a true economic democracy in America, are issuing self-righteous blasts against the Fascists that are a direct incitement to violence.

A war psychosis is being fostered by the very leaders of thought and action who should be the chief bulwarks against another war. If England and France and Russia are able to persuade us to fight their battles for them again it will be largely because of the aid of the pacifists and radicals who made the loudest outcry against our participation in the last war.

Since Spain is at the present time the danger spot of Europe, the scene of what is already virtually an international war, and most likely to be the immediate *casus belli*, it is of the utmost importance to get at the truth about Spain. At present there appears to be almost a conspiracy to prevent an honest understanding of Spain. Hysterical proponents make it appear that on one side there is nothing but a depraved and bestial sadism, while all heroism and goodness are in the other camp.

Before trying to answer, let us first consider the question of atrocities. Atrocities are not a reason for going to war, for going to war means going out to commit atrocities. The Germans sunk women and children on the *Lusitania,* so we helped starve a whole generation of German children. Spanish Loyalist airmen killed German sailors on the *Deutschland,* and in retaliation German sailors killed women and children in Almeria. In retaliation for this in turn many Americans are ready to kill more Germans, with the latest modern devices of mutilation and death. It is often suggested that there are rules of killing that ought to be observed. Malaga, Badajoz, Guernica, and now Almeria, are apparently atrocities without military objective. The answer is that in religious wars frightfulness always reaches new heights. Fascists believe that all "reds" are subhuman, compounded wholly of evil, and therefore to be exterminated without trace. The anti-Fascists are rapidly coming to the same irrational view of the Fascists. The next general war is not going to make nice distinctions between combatants and non-combatants, or between military and non-military objectives.

If more American liberals could wax sufficiently indignant to do something about the poverty into which our own slum children are born, then their indignation over those Spanish children who have suffered a comparatively merciful fate by bombing could be taken more seriously.

But if the reader will accept our conviction that atrocities in themselves are insufficient reason for risking involvement in war, there remains the second argument: how can American democracy fail to take sides when the democratically elected government of Spain is violently attacked by a minority, apparently mere reactionaries, supported by the dictator-

ships of Italy and Germany? While it is still possible, let us attempt to examine the economic and political factors behind the civil war objectively.

First of all, it is obvious that the Spanish monarchy of 1931 was a push-over for the young Republic. Weakly supported by a decadent church, an antiquated feudal aristocracy of the land, and certain large capitalistic interests (the majority of them foreign), King Alfonso's regime collapsed virtually without bloodshed within a year after its dummy strong-man, Primo de Rivera, abandoned it. Army and middle classes joined with radical and proletarian and peasant in the revolution. The true die-hards could rally no support. And it is significant that Queipo de Llano, now one of Franco's generals, together with a brother of Franco, flew over Madrid dropping leaflets proclaiming the Republic.

But the new Republic was bitterly divided against itself. Long tyranny had left the country too unsteady and divided for the compromises of a liberal democracy. Hot-headed individualism, conflicting extremes of radicalism, bitter antagonisms of economic interest, separatist tendencies in Catalonia and the Basque country, capitalism and socialism emerging almost simultaneously from feudalism and at once ready for internecine combat —all this meant that orderly, peaceful progress would be a miracle. The peasants and the middle classes held the balance of power: the peasantry because it represented the mass of voting strength; the middle classes because they were vocal and influential, and because the army —huge for a small country—was more likely to have a common interest with them in a "middle" course.

In the elections of 1933 the clash of forces led to the first impasse. The peasants had not been given the land reforms they prayed for in their churches, and they swung their support from the liberal republicans who had failed to carry out their promises over to the right, whose promises at least were still plausible. The reaction that followed was violent and cruel, and the slaughter of the Asturian miners in the 1934 uprising showed how far apart were the forces that had ousted Alfonso. The forces of the left, who wanted to make the revolution a real Revolution, a Socialist Revolution, had learned that they must combine, and that they must win allies. They formed the People's Front. They won back peasant support. They promised the Basques autonomy, and thus won the support of the conservative and Catholic Basque Nationalists. Anarchists, Socialists, former Trotskyists and dissident Marxists agreed to sink their differences for the time being. There were few Communists, but the influence of the Comintern was thrown behind the People's Front, for Communist policy was now to promote such reformist anti-Fascist movements.

The result was a triumph for the People's Front in the elections of February, 1936. Though its components only won a bare majority of the votes counted, 52 per cent, their seats in the Cortes were 277 to the rightists' 132 (total seats in the Cortes, 473).

All the groups which feared proletarian Socialism were now alarmed and aroused. A true Fascist movement, the *Falange Española,* which had not figured in the elections, began to grow among the middle classes and the army. The forces of reaction, the landowners, the industrialists, the bankers, and the upper ranks of the church and the army, plotted desperately. They believed, or professed to believe, that a "red uprising" was imminent, a Socialist revolution

against capitalism and against the church. There was much to justify their belief. The common people, feeling hated institutions crumbling, began to take the initiative against their age-old oppressors. They burned churches, pillaged monasteries that had become rich out of their toil and sweat. Peasants who had waited long enough for land began to take it. The government seemed weak. Its strongest backers were the Socialists led by Largo Caballero, left-wing Leninists unhampered by the present conciliatory policy of Moscow, waiting for the moment they had spent their lives preparing for. The power of the trade unions—the anarcho-syndicalist CNT, the Socialist UGT, the left Marxist (formerly Trotskyist) POUM—was mighty and growing. What more natural than for the conservatives to imagine "the worst," and try a desperate counter-attack before the enemy had time to move?

With the outbreak of the revolt the initial line-up began to change. The Rebels had most of the army, and they had the Fascist powers, Italy and Germany, to back them up. But this was not enough. They needed fighting men. The Italians sent in some, but they proved unreliable. The Germans confined themselves to experts and munitions. The Moors could be used as mercenaries, but they were not sufficient. Only the middle classes and the peasantry could furnish adequate cannon fodder. The middle classes were easy to win for an anti-Bolshevik crusade, and the *Falange Española* grew swiftly, furnishing the bulk of the Rebel militia. The peasantry, Catholic but anticlerical, land-hungry but individualistic, suspicious of city promises, was open to persuasion.

The peasants were, as a matter of fact, helplessly caught between two fires. In Loyalist territory they were treated with new respect, but they had to put up with requisitioning and collectivization and Socialist planners—and liquidation if they objected too much. In Rebel territory they were probably told they were defending their land and their religion from the Communist anti-Christ, but they were likely to find the landlord still on their necks; yet the huge rebel territory with its extended lines could not be held unless a substantial peasant support were available. This can hardly have been secured with threats alone, or promises alone.

The result of the struggle has been the transformation of the Rebellion from a mere revolt of reactionary groups to a real Fascist movement. Italian Fascist newspapers gibe at the Spanish grandees who have had to flee in the style of Haile Selassie. German aviators "save civilization from the Red Hordes" by dropping bombs on the Basque holy city. Fuehrer Franco declares a totalitarian state on "syndicalist" lines (i.e. "corporative" as in Italy). The Fascist Falange now claims 2,000,000 members, and absorbs one by one the old rightist parties, willy nilly.

Fascism as the preceding article of this series emphasized, is a form of collectivism. Whatever support it may have in the beginning from reactionary forces, it is subject to inner pressures—the political pressure of a mass movement that desperately wants and has been promised change, and the economic pressure of self-sufficient militarism—and these pressures force it to adopt more and more of the features of the system it professes to abhor. The collectivist dictatorships, Italy, Germany, and Russia come to look increasingly alike, approaching from opposite directions.

The Hearst press recently let slip the following obviously uninspired report from its star foreign correspondent, H. R.

Knickerbocker, then in London.

When I jokingly remarked to a group of Falangists in Salamanca that their Fascism was only Communism in another uniform they seriously replied: "Yes, Communism run by the right people."

Between the medievalism of Sanchez [an officer aristocrat] and the pro-labor, pro-peasant, anti-clerical, anti-capitalist, and anti-landlord Fascists, there exist on Franco's side men of every shade of opinion.

Franco's rebellion has become a Fascist movement. It is not only the reactionaries among its supporters who have misgivings. The "liberal" Catholics, for whom Michael Williams professes to speak in the *Commonweal,* "differ greatly in their economic and social ideals and aspirations from the rank reactionaries, and economic exploiters, and antiquated monarchists, and fanatical Fascists, with whom they are now uneasily associated." They do not like what is happening to their church in Nazi Germany.

On the other side changes have been occurring too. A people's army cannot be a parliamentary debating society. Foreign aid is essential, against the foreign aid Franco is getting. Soviet Russia alone feels able to help. Russian planes and Russian tanks are the answer to German and Italian planes and tanks. The influence of the Communists grows. Pictures of Stalin decorate Madrid houses. The red salute and the Internationale become the symbols of "the Revolution."

This is not due solely or even in large part to Russian influence, however. The compromise Republican regime which had collapsed immediately after the Revolt broke out—five cabinets in seven weeks—was followed by strong left Socialist government under Caballero. These Socialists were Leninists, but not necessarily Stalinists. Even farther left were the Anarchists and the POUM, who wanted the revolution to proceed at once to its conclusion, without waiting for the war to be won. The growing Communist movement combatted these extremist tendencies. The Comintern is in no hurry for world revolution—it feels it much more important to defeat Fascism, even if this requires an alliance with capitalist or middle-class forces for the time being.

The Communists seem finally to have won—though ironically enough their victory means the defeat of what their opponents think of as "Communism." Beginning with the outlawing of the "Trotskyist" POUM, the Government under Communist influence then had to put down—with blood—an anarchist uprising in Barcelona, which was using Catalan separatism as a lever against the "class-collaborationism" of the Valencia government. And finally Caballero was ousted. The new government, while outwardly moderate Republican, will carry through on the line advocated by the Communists: unified military command to win the war, a postponement of the socialist revolution (already churches are being reopened and confiscated property returned to its owners), and observance of democratic forms to assure the support of wide liberal support in the democratic countries.

In its international aspect, then, the Spanish Civil War is a struggle between the Fascist powers and the Soviet Union. If a general European war breaks out over the Spanish issue, it will be because those countries have decided the time has come to fight it out. England and France will be reluctantly drawn in, partly because their capitalist empires are threatened by Fascist aggression, and partly because their labor and radical movements are naturally anti-Fascist.

But this does not tell the whole story. Spain is not a mere pawn on the international chess-board. Her own people are fighting and dying on both sides, for what they believe in. Not all on the Fascist side are mercenaries or conscripts. Many are dying because they have been brought to believe that the "reds" aim to destroy all that they consider "civilization." Many of them doubtless believe their "nationalism" to be a nobler, more advanced form of radicalism than any international collectivism could possibly be. Many of them doubtless are inspired by the perverted decadent romanticism that makes up the ideology of Fascism everywhere.

On the other side of no-man's-land are forces, which, however divided and confused, cannot but arouse our enthusiasm and sympathy. There are to be found representatives of everything that progressive thought in America believes in. An oppressed people is struggling out of darkness, seeking freedom. Whether or not the devotion to democracy is altogether sincere on the part of those who now see the advocacy of democracy politically expedient, there can be no doubt that most of those who are dying for the republic are dedicated to democracy in the most sacred sense. The indications now available of the regeneration through which Loyalist Spain is already passing: the economic and social reforms, the spread of education, the fertile experimenting in agriculture and industry, most of all the fervid and joyous consecration which every observer has remarked there, as in every country at a time of profound and constructive revolutionary change—all these can leave no shadow of doubt that the People's Front in Spain does represent what we mean by "progress." This "progress" may be halted by the exigencies of war and political maneuvering. Democracy may be completely submerged in a dictatorship first imposed by military necessity. Social change may be delayed and perverted for immediate political advantage. The end result may be a pattern of the Soviet dictatorship, which, as indicated in the preceding article in this series, becomes startlingly like the Fascist foe whom it fights. But for the time being the heroism of Valencia and Madrid is the heroism of humanity's highest aspirations.

Yet how can those progressive forces in America whose aspirations are the same—economic and social liberation in a new social order—participate in that struggle? Some of more than common courage can go to Spain to fight, and die. Others can give aid of various kinds. But if the United States gets embroiled in another war that is another story. The stake is no longer Spain. The stake is no longer democracy. The stake can hardly be a new social order, except as war brings war collectivism, the type of army Socialism of which the Fascist nations are now the prototypes.

We must remain neutral. We must retain the chance we have to build on this continent, with our rich heritage, something new on earth: a true cooperative commonwealth, established on democracy because born in peace. The idea has been made current that new worlds, like new human beings, must be born in blood. The brood of dictatorships which has sprung from such grim origins is too much scarred and twisted by the process to reconcile us to that way if there is another.

If we would stay out of war, then, we must pay the price. Neutrality is not easy and it has no sure formula. But surely the risk involved in permitting munitions to be shipped "to the friendly government of Spain" is too great. Surely it is right for the government to impose, as it has, the limited protection of the new Neutrality Act. This action should go farther of course. The Fascist nations should be treated as already belligerents. The raw materials of war should be put on the forbidden list. Perhaps even the floods of foreign propaganda, whose only result can be to prepare us for war by throwing us emotionally off balance, should be curbed.

Above all the growing forces of progressivism in this country, on whose wisdom and courage the future of America depends, must see clearly, and learn the lessons of the Spanish conflict.

The most obvious lesson is that violence begets violence. "He that taketh up the sword shall perish by the sword." Centuries of brutal repression in Spain bred deep hatreds in the souls of the people. Their revolt was bound to be so violent that it would arouse terror and counter-revolt among all who feared to lose. And now 300,000 of the Spanish people have been murdered, because no statesmanship could be found inspired enough to unite those who wanted change.

The second problem then is to find a way to unite those who want to move forward. Fascism arises, insofar as one can isolate its origin, when the restless middle classes and the restless proletariat turn on each other rather than on their common foe, capitalism. In Spain, where the industrial workers numbered only 2,000,000 out of a population of nearly 30,000,000, a reliance on labor to achieve change left the great majority open to capture by the other side. A natural but unfortunate confusion of Catholicism with the grandees of the Catholic church enabled the opposition to raise the powerful symbol of the cross against the hammer and sickle.

Catholicism in America has been

driven by events in Spain, and by the attitude of American progressivism, to side with Franco. A little more and the vast influence of Catholicism will be assured to reaction and Fascism in the next American crisis. Yet, as Father Ryan, author of "A Better Economic Order," pointed out in *Common Sense* a year ago, just as the Spanish Civil War was getting under way, "The Catholic Church does not support or sanction the institution of Capitalism as it now operates." There is nothing advocated today by American Progressivism, or likely to be advocated by it, which could not be reconciled to the Papal Encyclicals on the social order. Let American Progressives beware how they drive twenty million American Catholics, whose need for fundamental change is as great as any, into the arms of a Coughlin or, worse yet, a Franco.

For the last four years America has taken the first awkward but nevertheless giant strides toward a new social order. If the march continues as it has begun, and if the leadership shifts more and more from those who have no clear understanding of the issue to those who know that production-for-use is the only answer, we may see a gradual but nonetheless swift elimination of our capitalist past. If we have peace, if we keep our hands to our own task, if we set our own house in order, we may be able to show a mad world the way to sanity. *But we must have peace.*

OPEN LETTERS

In the fall of 1937, the bishops of the Spanish Catholic Church sent forth a pastoral letter in which they told their side of the Spanish controversy. This letter was acrimoniously denounced in a number of denominational magazines of Protestant sects in America. A group of 150 American Protestants drafted a joint letter which severely criticized the Spanish bishops.

American Catholics accepted the challenge. They responded with an equally detailed defense of their Church and of the role of the Spanish bishops in the civil war. The two letters state the positions taken, in a thousand editorials, articles, and letters, by large numbers of American Protestants and Catholics. They dramatize the remarkably intense domestic antagonism which the Spanish Civil War engendered.

OPEN LETTER OF 150 PROTESTANTS

The text of the open letter issued by 150 Protestant clergymen and educators and laymen on the recent pastoral letter of the Spanish hierarchy follows:

The pastoral letter issued by the prelates of the Catholic Church in Spain stirs our anxieties. The Spanish hierarchy's attempt to justify a military rebellion against a legally elected government is alarming, as is its display of open hostility toward popular government, freedom of worship and separation

New York *Times*, October 4, 1937.

of church and State—principles that we, as Americans, deeply cherish.

Its apparent unwillingness to recognize the social and economic evils that have sickened Spain for generations is disquieting to those who feel that there can be no stability in the peninsula until these evils are eliminated; that resort again to force, repression and dictatorship can only be futile. In this respect the Spanish hierarchy will not admit what leading Catholics here and abroad have long discussed and deplored.

It is noteworthy that this pastoral letter was issued to answer criticism abroad of the Spanish hierarchy's position, criticism voiced not by the secular but by the Catholic press.

We are amazed to find the pastoral letter (1) approving of resort to violence and military insurrection as a means of settling political controversies; (2) rejecting not merely the present Popular Front Government of Spain but the republic itself and the Constitution of 1931 on which it was founded; (3) stigmatizing any form of parliamentary government, presumably even if under a constitutional monarchy as "irresponsible autocracy"; and (4) condemning in prin ciple the democratic institutions, the freedom of worship and the separation of church and state established by the Constitution of 1931. It is hard to believe that this pastoral letter was written in the twentieth century.

We do not question the right of the Spanish prelates to these beliefs. But when they voice these beliefs in an official appeal for world-wide support, they raise questions of grave import in every democratic country.

Is the Spanish hierarchy speaking for itself or for the Catholic Church as a whole? Does it have, as it claims to have, the sympathetic approval of the Vati can? Is it true, as the prelates state, that "there is nothing in the pastoral letter that is in contradiction with the view of the Vatican"?

If this is so, is this to be the policy of the Catholic Church in other democratic countries, where antecedents of the present Spanish struggle were fought to a conclusion centuries ago, and church and state permanently separated?

Does this pastoral letter, for example, reflect the political views of the Catholic Church in America? Certainly the contrast between the respected and secure position of the church in America and its troubles in Catholic Spain demonstrates conclusively that separation of church and state is as beneficial to the church as it is to the state.

Yet, we cannot help being disturbed by the fact that no leaders of the Catholic Church in America have raised their voices in repudiation of the position taken by the Spanish hierarchy. Quite the contrary, they, too, seem to have given their blessing to General Franco and his Fascist allies.

The attitude of the Spanish hierarchy on the use of force and violence is clearly expressed in the following terms: "Let it remain, therefore, established as the first assertion of this document . . . that the national conscience felt that once lawful legal means were exhausted, there was no other recourse left but that of violence for maintaining order and peace . . . through the fatal logic of the facts, Spain had no other alternative but this . . ."

We are at a loss to reconcile the approval thus given to the rebellion with the past stand of the Church, in Spain as elsewhere, in support of civil order and against the "unjust war" and violence. Indeed, many of the same prelates who signed this pastoral letter joined in the collective declaration of the Spanish Bishops of December, 1931, which said: "The Church never fails to teach submission and obedience as due to the constituted power, even when those who hold and represent that power use it in abuse of the Church." . . .

Today, however, the Spanish episcopate not only condones but actively supports a military revolt against a legitimate government. To excuse their inconsistency, the prelates offer an ingenious argument. They assert that the victory of the People's Front parties in the elections of February, 1936, came about "through governmental connivance which overrode the people's will, forming a political machine in conflict of the majority of the nation."

They then make the shocking declaration that "the war, therefore, is like an armed plebiscite." By such reasoning they attempt to convince the world of the respectability and legitimacy of the present rebellion.

If the war is simply a "plebiscite," are Franco's Nazis, Moors, and Italians then simply imported voters?

"What right have these foreign troops," asks Professor James T. Shotwell in the New York Times, "to cast their votes in the blood and iron ballots that blotted out Basque liberties?"

An "armed plebiscite" is an obvious absurdity, sinister in the contempt it reflects for democratic procedure. . . .

In attempting to nullify the Popular Front victory of 1936, [the hierarchy] is arrogating to itself a power superior to that of the Spanish Government and its Constitution. By so doing it is not only jeopardizing orderly and legal government, but promoting the very lawlessness of which it so bitterly complains.

Moreover, we believe that religion and the dignity of the church must suffer irreparably when its leaders become pawns in the game of politics.

The pastoral letter reveals that the Spanish episcopate, in attacking the Popular Front Government as Communistic, is actually voicing its opposition to any form of democratic government in Spain.

"We would be the first to regret," the prelates say, "that the irresponsible autocracy of a parliament should be replaced by the yet more terrible one of a dictatorship without roots in the nation."

Thus they speak of parliamentary government as "irresponsible autocracy." They seem, moreover, to oppose only certain kinds of dictatorships, those "without roots in the nation."

Does this mean that the Spanish hierarchy will rest content only when the republic has been overthrown, the Constitution repealed, the Bourbons restored and a new de Rivera dictatorship established?

That we do not exaggerate the hierarchy's intense dislike for republican institutions is proved elsewhere in the pastoral letter. It reveals its real antipathy when it says: "The Constitution and the secularist laws which developed its spirit were a violent and continuous attack against the national conscience."

What, in effect, does this mean? It can only mean that the Spanish episcopate is still fundamentally opposed to freedom of worship (which the Constitution of 1931 guaranteed to all citizens for the first time in Spain's history); to separation of church and State; to the placing of education in the hands of the State; to agrarian reform. For these are among the things that the Constitution and the secularist laws made secure. . . .

The part taken, or supposedly taken,

by the Soviet Union is emphasized to an extent far beyond the testimony of even the most anti-Loyalist newspaper correspondents. Yet the Spanish prelates do not so much as have one word about the aid given Franco by the Nazis, the Italians, and the Moors. On the contrary, we are told that "the Nationalist movement has released a current of love which has concentrated round the name and historical essence of Spain, with aversion for the foreign elements who occasioned our ruin."

Presumably, the reference to "foreign elements" here is to the Soviet Union and not to the Nazi bombers who poured fire and destruction on the women and children of Madrid, Durango, Guernica, Malaga, and Almeria.

We are led to believe that the whole "Nationalist" uprising was inspired to forestall a seizure of power under the direction of the "Russian Comintern." There is no evidence in the pastoral letter to substantiate this serious charge.

We cannot but observe with amazement the Spanish hierarchy's appeal to the "law of nations" in a situation where the German and Italian allies of General Franco have disregarded and violated at random the most solemn precepts of international law. This appeal is marked by the same partisan treatment of the actualities which characterized the entire pastoral letter.

The Spanish hierarchy shows itself equally indifferent to the actual facts, as attested by impartial and even Catholic observers, when it passes over the evidence of systematic brutality and religious persecution on the Rebel side. M. Jacques Maritain, whom even the London *Tablet,* the well-known Catholic organ, calls "balanced and soundly orthodox," has raised his voice in protest against the frightful massacre of Loyalists by the Rebels at Badajoz.

"It is sacrilege," says M. Maritain, "to shoot, as at Badajoz, hundreds of men to celebrate the Feast of the Assumption."

Several thousand words are devoted to a description of alleged atrocities by the Loyalists. But of those on the Rebel side all the pastoral letter says is "every war has its excesses; the Nationalist movement may have had them also; nobody defends himself with full serenity from the mad attacks of a pitiless enemy." Not one word about the murder of priests and nuns in Rebel territory, of the systematic destruction of the Protestant missions which have grown up in Spain since the republic was established, of the execution of many Protestant ministers by the Rebels, of the destruction of the religious sanctuary of Begona in the Basque country. . . .

We do not deny, and we join the hierarchy in deploring the excesses which have occurred on the Loyalist side, but in all fairness the fact must be recorded that these excesses have been attributable to irresponsible elements and that the Madrid regime has made every effort to prevent such violence and punish those responsible. . . .

Violence on the Rebel side has not been mob violence. It has been violence deliberately directed by the military-Fascist leaders.

Nor do we expect clerics who are themselves on the territory of and in the power of the Franco regime, to discuss objectively the religious toleration provided for by law on Loyalist territory, as contrasted with the fact that Franco allows religious liberty only to Catholics sympathetic to Fascism.

The attitude of the Rebel leadership

toward civil and religious liberties was plainly, if unpleasantly stated by General Miguel Cabanellas of the Rebel high command and former president of the Burgos junta.

"Our enemy," he said, "is a strange company of ordinary criminals, anarchists, communists, illiterates and prostitutes. . . . Spain will be governed in a fashion which will make it impossible for power ever again to fall in the hands of dirty politicians, Freemasons and similar parasites of human society."

The general was but elaborating on a statement made by Gil Robles, leader of Catholic Action, when he said, in 1933, "We shall clean Spain of Masons and Jews."

We think it extremely regrettable that religion should have been made an issue in the rebellion. It is clear that the Span-

ish conflict is between the forces of democracy and social progress, on the one hand, and the forces of special privilege and their Fascist allies, on the other.

Mussolini even publicly boasts of the fall of Santander as an achievement of his Black-shirt Fascists.

It is unfortunate that the Spanish hierarchy should thus be made to appear as the apologists for reaction and fascism. We are loath to believe that this pastoral letter definitely expresses the position of the Catholic Church on the armed rebellion against, and the Fascist invasion of, Republican Spain.

Certainly the hierarchy can hardly expect to gain sympathy here either for itself or for the Catholic religion with a declaration that treats with contempt principles that are the precious heritage of the American people.

AMERICAN CATHOLICS REPLY

The outbreak on July 18, 1936, of the military conflict in Spain has precipitated a situation in which there is daily danger of a conflict between the major nations of the world. There has been precipitated likewise a clash of ideologies in the minds of every intelligent observer of world events. Hence it is essential for the preservation of world peace that the facts in the Spanish situation, the ideologies of the contending forces and the causes which lead up to the present deplorable condition should be truly and accurately understood by every American.

Even those who had been close students of Spanish affairs, especially since the establishment of the Republic in 1931, were shocked by the suddenness and by the violence of the outbreak of the Civil

War. The Government then resident at Madrid was the established power in Spain. For that reason it had the assumption of authority, an authority which was being disputed by an insurgent element. It had moreover at its disposal diplomatic channels for communication with the governments of the world. In addition to this it had an officially established department of propaganda for the dissemination of reports favorable to itself. As a result the foreign governments and the foreign press were disposed to favor the Madrid Government and to condemn outright those who were immediately designated as rebels.

It was only in succeeding months after battles had been fought and campaigns executed, that the true issues of the conflict precipitated on July 18 were clari-

"Catholics Reply to Open Letter of 150 Protestant Signatories on Spain," *Catholic Mind,* XXXV (November 22, 1937), pp. 453–465.

fied. During the latter part of the summer and autumn of 1936 it was possible to learn of the conditions that brought about an armed uprising, to be aware of the governmental, economic, social, and religious principles that animated the combatants. Before all the facts about Spain during the year 1936 were fully disclosed, the Madrid Government was able to enlist the sympathies of the people with democratic instincts in the democratic countries of the world.

In the United States the cause of the Madrid Government was popularized through the newspapers, through the support of liberal and radical elements, and through the direct help of Communistic organizations. The result was a bitter and vehement detestation of the Nationalists in Spain, a campaign of misrepresentation, errors, and deliberate lies. This condition has been changed more and more since the early months of 1937. The facts about Spain and the issues involved in Spain have been more honestly and honorably publicized, and hence they should be understood by those who uphold civic and religious freedom for all men.

Since these facts and issues covering both the Loyalist and Nationalist parties in the Spanish Civil War are known, it is not only surprising but gravely alarming to find that there are 150 Protestant clergymen and laymen who were willing to sign the document published in the New York *Times* for October 4th, under the heading *An Open Letter in Reply to Spanish Hierarchy's Recent Views of War*. The publication of that letter has not only misrepresented the facts and the issues of Spain, but it has also tended to create a species of religious war in the United States.

Though the signatories of this present reply to the Open Letter are accepting the challenge contained in the letter signed by the 150 Protestant clergymen and laymen, the challenge in reality is to American Protestantism. Specifically, the challenge is this: Do American Protestants accept and endorse a governmental regime that is composed predominantly of radical Socialists, Communists, Syndicalists, and Anarchists? Does American Protestantism champion a regime that has consistently violated in theory and in practice the fundamental principles of liberty and democracy guaranteed by the Constitution of the United States?

It is not necessary for any Protestant or any Catholic to give his complete approbation to the Nationalist cause in Spain. But it is absolutely and unquestionably necessary for every Protestant and Catholic in the United States to repudiate and to condemn the policies and the acts against religious and civic liberty perpetrated by the so-called Loyalist Government.

It seems to us well, then, to present a true statement in regard to the conflict in Spain and correction of the errors contained in the Open Letter of the 150 Protestant signatories.

It cannot be emphasized too strongly that the conflict in Spain is civil, primarily, and religious, secondarily. The war that lamentably now rages is between those who attempted through governmental changes to force on the Spanish people a Sovietized or anarchized regime and those who resisted that attempt. The Catholic citizens of Spain, both clerical and lay, aligned themselves with General Franco as Spanish citizens and not as Catholics. The Spanish citizen as a citizen had an immediate and tragic decision to make on July 18, 1936, for or against a governmental administration that had persecuted the citizens civilly and also as

Catholics. The decision was for or against a political group that had seized power and was professedly and energetically aspiring to the Sovietization of Spain, that was gradually, yet with purpose and foresight, building up a dictatorship, that would repress the individualistic as well as the social aspirations of the Spanish citizens as citizens.

The moderate elements in Spanish life, both those of the Left and of the Right wing, all the parties of the Right and a very great percentage of the industrial and agricultural classes found that their essential liberties were being violated, that their public and parliamentary protests against governmental encroachments of liberty and life were being disregarded. Their discontent with the Government on the social and economic basis was such that they would welcome the leadership of anyone who would relieve them of the slavery that was being forced upon them. Those in Spain who are giving their support to and fighting on the side of the Nationalists are citizens who are attempting to release themselves from a regime which would corrupt the national soul and would deprive them as citizens of the blessings of true liberty and democracy guaranteed to them by the Spanish Republic.

When in 1931 the Monarchy was peacefully abolished and the Republic was gloriously established, the Hierarchy, the clergy, and the Catholic citizens of Spain not only accepted it but loyally threw into it all of their ability and enthusiasm. Almost immediately upon the establishment of the Republic, however, the Communist and radical elements introduced a spirit of disharmony with the Spanish character. The Communist and radical elements had for years been propagandizing in Spain and preparing for the day of revolution. They seized upon the first Cortes and immediately built up their political power. However, Catholics both as Spanish citizens and as Spanish Catholics cooperated with the successive governments and strove to further a progressive and liberal program for the good of the Spanish people. Between 1931 and February, 1936, there is not a single instance of Catholics as Catholics taking any action that was in violation of civil or religious liberty. During those same years there are countless instances of the Communist, Syndicalist, and Anarchist elements using suppressive and reprehensive measures against their fellow-citizens and inciting them to rebellion, as in the revolt of the Asturians in 1934.

During the period of 1931–32, the very time during which the new Spanish Constitution was drawn up and promulgated, the XII Plenum of the Executive Committee of the Communist International was held in Moscow. The theses adopted included the statement that "the prerequisites for a revolutionary crisis are being created at a rapid pace in Spain." The record for Spain during the succeeding years fully justified this claim.

As 1931 saw a critical turn in Spanish history, so February, 1936, was a critical month in the history of the Spanish Republic. It has been stated time and time again that the popular majority in the February elections went to the Rightist front, but that the electoral laws, through previous manipulation on the part of the Leftist majority in the Cortes, threw the majority representation to Leftist deputies. The majority was of the slightest, but it gave the Leftist deputies the legal power further to manipulate the results through secondary elections. A larger majority for the Left in the Cortes was, therefore, secured. The Catholic citizens of Spain and the parties of the Right accepted the result of the election, though with protest, and attempted continued cooperation with the Government in power.

This Government, however, feeling its strength, began to take active measures whereby the opposing parties would be so weakened politically that they would be unable ever again to form into a concerted opposition. It either instigated or connived at the suppression of religious liberty and the destruction of religious edifices, at the suppression of freedom of speech and public opinion in and out of Parliament, at the suppression of freedom of the press through the destruction of newspapers and periodicals. More than that, as authoritative documents show, it was preparing for a military coup for the seizure of absolute power in the late spring or early summer of 1936. The decision of the Government, strongly Communistic, was the usurpation of governmental agencies supported by lawless military agencies for the perpetuation of a radical Leftist regime.

Calvo Sotelo, the parliamentarian who warned Spain that after a victory in the February elections for the United Front "there would wave over Spain the Red flag, the symbol of the destruction of Spain's past, her ideals and her honor," was murdered on July 13, 1936. The patriots of Spain, after their proposals to the permanent committee of the Parliament had been rejected, realized with finality that the crisis had come. All legitimate peaceful, parliamentary, and electoral methods of changing the government or securing justice from the Government had failed. There was no alternative except recourse to arms.

Catholics are against war, and more especially against civil war. Catholics hate war, seek for its ultimate abolition, and insist that disputes shall be settled as far as is humanly possible by pacific means. But when war is brought to them, when war is the only recourse against an oppressive minority in power, when there is no alternative between war and the loss of all that men hold sacred in the way of liberty and life, then Catholics, as did the Catholics of Spain, must save themselves from destruction and annihilation. The citizens of Spain, therefore, were justified by the right of self-defense in rising up against a malign power that was surely and inevitably destroying their country. Those who would deny them the exercise of this inalienable right would with equal logic have denied to the American people in 1776 the exercise of their inalienable right to rebel in arms against a government which suppressed their liberties.

The extreme—and inexplicable—reluctance of the various protesters to bear even a passing mention of Communistic activities cannot conceal the fact the governmental chaos was utilized to the utmost effect by a methodical and concerted activity emanating from the Soviet Government in Russia.

In the words of Paul Claudel, former Ambassador of France to the United States, a man world-known for his temperance and liberality of judgment: "All those forces of destruction"—governmental incapacity, Soviet anti-religion, and anarchistic destructiveness—"unchained themselves with a frightful violence." "It is impossible to understand," says Claudel, "the Spanish Revolution, which came to a complete head in 1936, unless one sees in it, not an attempt at social construction, as in Russia, with the idea of substituting one order for the other, but an enterprise of destruction, long prepared and guided, particularly against the Church."

The significance of these attacks upon religion lies not alone in their incredible violence, but in the extreme thoroughness, the minuteness with which all the churches within the Communist regions were set on fire, all religious objects minutely destroyed, and practically all the priests and Religious massacred with unheard of refinements of cruelty. They bear the unmistakable evidence of being the work of a "conscious and fanatical minority," which with cold intelligence made use of the passions of the mob.

The attempt to represent the Communist activities in Spain as the sequel or consequence of the Insurgent movement is a perversion of facts which cannot stand up before the evidence of history. This activity had made its appearance repeatedly in the past, and preceded the civic-military uprising during four months of chaos prior to the February elections. Jesus Hernandez, Minister of Education to the Caballero Government, was able to report in June, 1936, that "the United Front has been organized in a thousand different forms and the driving force behind the whole movement is the Communist party . . . working illegally."

The civic-military movement, say the Bishops, and the Communist revolution "are two facts which cannot be separated if one wishes to form a fair judgment on the nature of the war." Moreover—a point completely overlooked by their critics—"the movement did not take place without those who initiated it previously urging the public authorities to oppose by legal means the imminent Marxian revolution. The attempt was unsuccessful. Russia has grafted herself onto the Government's army."

The Bishops sum up the situation in a word that is confirmed by documented evidence and the testimony of unprejudiced observers: "A shrewd organization put at the service of a terrible purpose of annihilation, concentrated against the things of God, with the modern means of movement and destruction within the reach of every criminal hand."

Completely misleading is the presentation of the anti-religious and anarchistic uprisings as the natural consequence of deep popular resentment created by social abuses. That such social abuses existed, that they were a contributory factor in the terrible situation in Spain, no reasonable person will deny. But it is a striking fact that the fiercest outbursts of violence and destruction took place not in those parts of Spain where want and social exploitation were most prevalent, but in Spain's most prosperous regions, where social works were active and the upward path toward industrial and agrarian reform had already been vigorously set on foot.

Such resentment as existed offered the ready field for agitators, for skilful propagandists of discontent. But the organization of this discontent, its utilization for the purposes of a planned attack upon religion and civic liberty was the work not of popular instinct, but of an agitation planned from without.

There is a fundamental assumption in the minds of the 150 signatories and probably in the minds of the majority of the American people who have been affected by propaganda, that the Loyalist Government is now the legitimate Government in Spain. This is an assumption and purely an assumption, not a matter of fact. The Government now operating at Valencia is not the Government that was elected in February, 1936, and does not profess the same policies as that Government or stand upon the mandate that was given to it by the vote of less than one-half the citizens of Spain in February, 1936. The Government elected at that time represented itself as a moderate Left-Wing Government. The successive premiers who were designated by a harassed and menaced Cortes were progressively Leftist and finally became Communist under Premier Largo Caballero. Certainly not one of the 150 signatories, nor any honest man, can assert that the Spanish people would give a majority to a Communist regime.

Due to internal troubles between the Stalinite Communists, the Trotskyite Communists, and the Syndicalists and the Anarchists there has been a conflict between the Leftist parties, and this conflict has not been settled by parliamentary methods but by use of force and repression. The present incumbent, Premier Negrin, has secured his power by the forcible ousting without parliamentary recourse of Largo Caballero and the more radical elements.

The Government now headed by Negrin cannot in any way be said to represent the will of the Spanish people. The Negrin Government cannot claim that it has the support of two-thirds of the Spanish people, or that it can exercise its jurisdiction over two-thirds of the Spanish land. The factual truth is that the Government elected in February, 1936, has ceased to exist. In its place have arisen two *de facto* governments battling for supremacy. More than that, by popular acceptance of leadership, one-third of Spain is held under the domination of Premier Negrin, and two-thirds of Spain has freely and enthusiastically acclaimed loyalty and allegiance to General Franco.

Two-thirds of the Spanish fighting force of their own volition are fighting under the standard of the Nationalists, and far less than one-third are willing to fight under the standard of Negrin. If an election were held tomorrow throughout all of Spain, an overwhelming popular vote would freely be given to General Franco, and a miserable minority would be accorded to Premier Negrin. The Spanish people have expressed themselves voluntarily and forcefully. They have repudiated in the only manner that is possible to them the Caballero and Negrin governments. Let foreigners, therefore, who hold to the principle of self-determination within nations, cease to meddle in the internal and domestic affairs of a free and independent people.

From the critical days of late July, 1936, the foreign press has been filled with propagandistic misrepresentations emphasizing the help given to the Nationalist cause by the Moors, Italians, and Germans, and has been strangely silent about the help given to the Loyalist cause by the Russians, the French, the dissident Germans, Italians, Czechoslovakians, and even Americans. In the matter of foreign intervention there has been a suppression of truth and the most vehement dissemination of untruths.

In regard to the Moors, it should be clear to everyone by this time that the Moors are as much citizens of Spain as are the Negroes citizens of the United States; that the Moors are as legitimately a part of the Spanish army as the well-respected Negro regiments are of the American army. No one will deny that German mechanics and strategists, and that Italian warriors are fighting for General Franco. But that is half of the story. The 150 signatories if they were honest would also affirm that Frenchmen from the very beginning have been supplying aviators, strategists and warriors to the Loyalists, that Russians have been directing the military maneuvers of the Loyalist army, have been piloting the planes that have brought destruction on Nationalist territory, and have been supplying money and munitions of all sorts for the Loyalist armies. In addition,

Americans in great numbers have been fighting as pilots and ground soldiers in two American brigades. The 15th Division of the Loyalist Army is composed of foreign interventionists.

Let all those foreign volunteers be withdrawn from Spain and let all foreign aid, governmental and unofficial, be cut off from Spain; segregate this war and let it remain a civil war between the citizens of Spain for their own self-determination and survival. If that were done the issues that are being fought out with bullets and bloodshed would quickly clarify themselves. If that were done the last day of the war would arrive quickly. Spain with its contending forces would then be able to right itself and to express itself. It is foreign intervention that is prolonging the agony and the crucifixion of Spain.

It is not surprising to find reference to Badajoz in the Open Letter of the 150 signatories. But it is surprising that men of integrity, who should know the facts, instance this discredited story. It is common knowledge that the story of Badajoz appeared in the Paris newspapers two days before the massacre at Badajoz was alleged to have taken place. Yet always, when speaking of atrocities, the hostile critics of the Nationalists fling forth the magic word "Badajoz."

Granted that there were executions in Badajoz, do they justify or do they lessen the guilt of the Loyalist Government in executing at least 14,000 priests and Religious in the territory of Spain held by them? Do they justify the murder or the execution of every prominent Rightist Catholic and non-Catholic in the cities and towns held by the Loyalists, since the opening of the war and before that? Do they justify the fully coordinated and authenticated murder of the families, including women and children, by way

of reprisals of Nationalist sympathizers?

Our position is not that of condoning murder or of exculpating the Nationalist authorities in atrocities whatever they may be, or in mass executions, or in any other violation of natural and divine law. Murder is always murder no matter who commits it. Cruelty is always cruelty no matter by whom perpetrated. But in this Spanish Civil War, as in all wars, the record of both sides must in honesty be drawn up. That record is lengthier and more inhuman on the side of the Loyalists than it is on the side of the Nationalists. The 150 signatories of the Open Letter would close their lips on the subject of the dehumanized atrocities of the Loyalists and insincerely cry out in condemnation of the alleged atrocities of the Nationalists.

As has been clearly pointed out in the statement by prominent British Protestants, published in the New York *Times* for October 7, the assertion that Protestant churches have been suppressed in the Nationalist territory is false. Not only have explicit guarantees been given as to the freedom of Protestant worship, but the Protestant church and schools in Salamanca have recently been restored to Protestants since Franco gained power in that city.

In the Open Letter of the 150 signatories there is a grave misrepresentation of the position held by the Spanish bishops, and in their expression of this position in the joint pastoral which aroused the ire of the Protestant clergymen and laymen. It may be stated categorically that the Spanish bishops in 1931 accepted the establishment of the Spanish Republic as an expression of the will of the Spanish people. The Spanish bishops accepted and gave allegiance to the Constitution drawn up by the first Cortes though reserving their right as Spanish citizens to question certain sections of this document. The Spanish bishops have accepted and favored the democratic and republican institutions in Spain. They have co-operated in the political, social, economic progress under the parliamentarian form of government in Spain. They have not had any other activities nor mingled in political issues nor become pawns of a political party. They have nobly championed the fundamental rights of man and the rights of all classes within the democracy, aristocratic, bourgeois, and proletarian. They have shown themselves to be deeply concerned with the eradication of social, and economic abuses and evils. They have been eager for the establishment of a regime of social justice, for popular education, for peace. The Spanish bishops have discovered, as have the citizens of Spain discovered, that they have been deceived and coerced by a minority group which seized the Government of republican Spain. After the election of 1936, the Spanish bishops clearly discerned, as did the citizens of Spain, that democracy has disappeared from the Loyalist side and that democracy will never return through a victory of the Loyalist Army. Spain, should General Franco and the Nationalists be defeated, will be turned into a Soviet Russia or will descend into a governmental category lower than Soviet Russia, a state of anarchy and chaos.

That the Church in Spain is in any way committed to the governments, the ideology, or the policies of Nazi or Fascist auxiliaries who have been helping the cause of Franco in Spain is a proposition entirely at variance not only with the Bishops' letter but with the facts as well. As was pointed out by Monsignor Ready in his letter of October 6 to the New York *Times*, the critics have completely twisted the obvious meaning of the Bishops' plain words in this regard when they write: "We would be the first to regret that the irresponsible autocracy of a parliament should be replaced by the yet more terrible one of a dictatorship, without roots in the nation."

Finally, we flatly deny as is asserted that this is a war between democracy and special privilege. The principles for which the Spanish bishops stand are the principles common to all humanity. They are the principles enunciated by George Washington and the founders of the American Republic and embodied in our democratic laws and institutions: the freedom to worship God in peace, freedom to educate one's children according to the dictates of one's conscience, freedom from the interference and tyranny of foreign states and alien agitators.

The Spanish bishops, as intelligent men, as true Christians, have called forth from the depths of their souls to intelligent and God-fearing men, whether these profess Catholicism or Protestantism or Judaism, for aid and understanding. They are men who have seen with their own eyes the hatred and class violence engendered by the closed fist, the materialism and atheism fostered under the symbol of the sickle and hammer. They are the men who seek a Spain that shall be the traditional Spain of courtesy and spirituality but also the new Spain with a progressive and equitable order of social and economic and political justice. They are the men who should be championed by the ministers of religion whether these be Catholic, Protestant, or Jewish. They are not the men who should be calumniated and attacked by Protestant clergymen.

The Spanish bishops have protested as men, as citizens, as Christians against a world propaganda that would aid and abet the destroyers of their social, religious, and national life. Their cause is not the cause of Catholics alone, nor yet of Christians alone, but of all men who believe in social and international peace and the moral law. The least we can do is to afford them a respectful hearing, and not heap them with abuse.

From The Commonweal: CIVIL WAR IN SPAIN AND THE UNITED STATES

Until June of 1938, the Catholic Worker, *an anarchist monthly, was the only Catholic periodical to remain neutral on the Spanish Civil War. All others supported the Nationalists. George Shuster, editor of the* Commonweal, *had, however, doubts about General Franco which he had expressed in two articles in April of 1937. On June 24, 1938, the* Commonweal *announced a change in its appraisal of the Spanish war.*

1. THE REASON FOR THIS STATEMENT

MOST discussion of the Spanish question to date in the United States by supporters of both sides has been distinguished more for its heat than for any light cast upon the significance of events. Those directly responsible for the conduct of this magazine have believed that anything they said, however temperate and however qualified as their own opinion, might add rather to the heat than to the light. We have hoped for peace, and the opportunity to comment upon the better problems which peace proposes. But the war continues, and the manner of waging it, both in Spain and here in our own country, seems to change very little with the passage of time. As long as "total" war continues on the Spanish peninsula, it will continue to torment all of us, both in America and in Europe.

We do not for an instant pretend that what is said below is the only proper position for Catholics in the matter; we only affirm our belief, subject to correction, that our position is perfectly compatible with Catholic principles and that it is a view shared by many thousands of American Catholics.

2. THE SPANISH PROBLEM IN SPAIN

First of all we feel that some distinction must be made between the Spanish problem *in Spain* and the Spanish problem *in the United States*. In Spain there is an active civil war which is being fought by both sides in order to achieve, from the point of view of each political group, a better social order. The same struggle to achieve a better social order exists in every country but not in the form of an *armed* struggle, of a civil war. The general problem exists throughout the world, but the war in Spain relates to Spaniards *acting* in their immediate struggle and allegiance; outside Spain it relates to non-Spaniards *observing* a more remote armed struggle and en-

From "Civil War in Spain and in the United States," *The Commonweal*, XXVIII (June 24, 1938), pp. 229–230.

gaged in the general problem in a different way.

We do not feel qualified to discuss the problem as it is in Spain in any detail because the information available is so generally characterized by propaganda that we do not have any sufficient knowledge of the whole situation. Two reports on a single event emanating from the opposing camps will be in complete contradiction to each other. The official principles of each side must be taken into account, but the actions of each side, when they can be known, speak louder than words.

A Spaniard, unless he is one of the few who are determined—and able—to make the "double refusal," seemingly must choose between two governments whose characters are mixed and are impossible to know from here with any comprehensiveness.

One government, or part of it, has instigated, or at least permitted, the murder of priests, nuns, and lay people; has utilized ruthless methods of accomplishing social and political and economic ends, and chosen, as far as it is possible to see, many objectives in all these fields that should be condemned. Its alliance with Russia implies some, if an unknown, degree of identification with the evils of the Soviet régime.

The second government, which gives the Church open support, yet, in its conduct of warfare, repeatedly and despite protests from the Holy Father, destroys defenseless civilians, particularly by its air raids upon cities. Air raids made by one side cannot cancel out those made by the other. Many of its leaders give utterance to totalitarian views very similar to those which have been condemned by the Church in other countries. The system of government it utilizes and favors, so far as can be seen, contains elements that should be sharply rejected. Its alliance with the Fascist and Nazi nations implicates it to some, if an uncertain, extent in the evils of those régimes. Of course, both Spanish governments are in a state of war, which of necessity, under any régime, imposes certain limitations on human freedom. The choice is, to our way of thinking, tragic, however much analogous choices have been necessary in the past and seem almost to be, from time to time, inevitable in man's political life.

What is the duty of Americans toward Spaniards in their present trouble? There is, of course, the obligation of alleviating distress and suffering on both sides, as much as lies in our power. There is the obligation of doing everything we can for peace. And there is the greatest obligation of all—the universal obligation of prayer for all the human souls involved in the conflict.

3. THE PROBLEM IN AMERICA

But there is a further obligation—that of learning what we can from the crucial struggle in Spain for use in the constant efforts we must make to achieve a better social order in our own country. There are two attitudes we can take in attempting to fulfill this obligation.

We can conceive the struggle for a better social order as inevitably taking in one's own country a pattern similar to that which it has taken in Spain. This usually involves whole-hearted partizanship for one side or the other in the Spanish war. It is the warm and emotional way of looking at the matter; it is the way which has been embraced by most American organs of opinion.

Or else we can try to learn from the Spanish war what to do in order to avoid the things on both sides of that conflict which seem incompatible with the achievement of a better society, and in order to carry on the developments necessary here without precipitating the carnage and hate engendered by war. This is, viewed superficially, an unappealing way of looking at the matter, and invites accusations of barren intellectualism, of indifference toward the truth. Yet we believe it is the charitable way, the rational and human way. It is not an attempt to achieve negative neutrality, which denies the existence of absolute right, but a positive impartiality: a search for the right, unblinded by that passionate partizanship which simplifies the problems that confront us to the dimensions of a slogan, and claims the right as the complete and exclusive possession of one warring party.

In this country there has been violent partizanship either for the Spanish Nationalists or for the Madrid-Barcelona government. We feel that violent American partizanship on either side with regard to the Spanish question is bad, not only because the facts are obscure, but chiefly because both sides include elements that no American wants imported into this country. Neither has begun to enforce or even propound anything comparable to the Bill of Rights, which protects an individual from unbearable abuse of authority.

It is alleged by his supporters that Franco is not a fascist, but a restorer of order; by its supporters that Madrid is not opposed to Christianity, but only to "political Catholicism." Since both allegations emanate from partizan sources, they are subject to serious question. But the fact remains that one section of the American public has been convinced that Franco is a fascist; another section has equally been convinced that the Madrid government is atheist and communist. *In the United States* the practical effect of being unreservedly and uncritically pro-Nationalist is to *seem* to one's fellow Americans pro-fascist; of being pro-Government is to *seem* pro-communist and anti-religious. The result is to intensify and to make more effectively dangerous both genuine fascism and communism in the United States.

To be strongly partizan concerning the Spanish Civil War is indeed to aggravate a current intellectual disease: the conviction that we are going to be forced to choose between fascism and communism. This is a dangerous disease; sufferers from it are blinded by it to the truth that both systems are anti-Christian and secularist. (Unquestionably the greatest error is to think that the life of Christianity is bound up with the maintenance of any such temporal form of society.) The choice today is between secularism, the Hegelian state in any of its current forms, and the "personalist" Christian state, conceived as existing for the protection and assistance of its citizens. The issue is, of course, never clear in any given instance; but to transfer the issue from its proper ground—the distinction between the conception of man as free and the conception of man as existing only by favor of the state—to a totally improper ground is to further the cause of evil. The freedom that demands the constant vigilance and protection of every citizen is the freedom to pursue a person's spiritual, *mental,* and social life without dictation by the exterior material force of a majority or a directing minority.

4. THE TACTIC AGAINST TOTALITARIAN SECULARISM

We are quite frankly whole-hearted partizans of the personalist, Christian state. The seeds of both fascism and communism will germinate only in the soil of injustice, and then must be fertilized by a general public conviction that the leaders of the non-totalitarian state are deficient in moral strength and do not deserve the confidence of their people.

The problem of preserving or creating a form of state in which Christianity can truly flourish is therefore primarily a moral problem and one internal to the country concerned. In each instance both the government and all citizens must dedicate themselves to remedying present injustices, solving present social and economic problems, and, as much as is possible, preventing future injustice. Those entrusted with the governance of the state must strive in every way to make themselves worthy of public confidence and trust.

In more homely words, the best because the only effective way to fight anti-Christian totalitarianism is to make one's own country a thoroughly decent place to live in, to "restore all things in Christ."

It is for these reasons that we believe that the wisest, as also the most charit-

able and perhaps the most difficult, policy for Americans is to maintain that "positive impartiality," a sanity of judgment toward both sides in Spain, expressing a preference for specific ideas and actions when they are certainly known, but being an uncritical partizan of neither. Americans should cease labeling everything they may not like in America or elsewhere as either "fascist" or "communist"; they should try, instead, to study American problems not only in the hope of contributing to their reasonable and equitable solution but also in the belief that such a solution in America will constitute a part of the solution of international and world problems. Above all, we must avoid fostering the growth of totalitarianism and hatred of Christianity by avoiding all activities that even faintly encourage that spirit of hysterical opposition and human distrust which is the very life blood of both of those systems. Peace can come only where there is good-will, and when there is good-will, the road is open to peace.

Michael Williams: VIEWS AND REVIEWS

The editors of the Commonweal *were not unanimous. Michael Williams had, in 1937, written a series of "Open Letters" in which he accused the secular press of willfully distorting the news from Spain. Faced now with a change in the policy of his own magazine, Williams objected strenuously. His objections were echoed by many Catholic journals horrified at the* Commonweal's *apostasy.*

THERE are so many important things well said in the statement on Spain made by the editorial directors of the *Commonweal* with which I heartily

agree, that my strong disagreement with the statement as a whole becomes painful and regrettable. I dislike the necessity of being personal in what I have to

From "A Dissent from Editorial Policy," by Michael Williams, *The Commonweal*, XXVIII (June 24, 1938), pp. 241–242.

say, but it seems necessary, under the circumstances. For of course I must suppose that the readers of this journal cannot help but recall the fact that when I was the editor, a year ago, I often and strongly expressed my belief that the armed revolt of the Franco forces in Spain, abhorrent as nearly all revolts against constituted authority must be for all who hold the teachings of the Catholic Church, was, under the circumstances existing in Spain, thoroughly justified; and that, because of those circumstances, the victory of the Franco uprising would be beneficial to the cause of Christian civilization; its defeat, therefore, disastrous to that cause in Spain itself, and a weakening of that cause elsewhere in the world, our own country, of course, included. I still hold those opinions; but the present editors of the *Commonweal* do not. Naturally, I am sorry for that fact; but it is quite clear that my personal feelings, as such, are irrelevant; the one important consideration is the question whether or not the advice now tendered to the *Commonweal* readers, namely, to be absolutely neutral, as concerns any judgments made upon the comparative merits of the contending forces, tends to be helpful or harmful to the interests of Christian civilization. For my own part, then, I am most regrettably constrained to say that such advice tends to be harmful.

My chief reason for thinking so is the fact (as it seems to me) that the *Commonweal's* statement carries its suspicion, and its repudiation, of the "propaganda" emanating from both sides in Spain far beyond a justifiable degree, and, therefore, it seems to ignore what to my way of thinking is the determining, ultimate truth concerning the Spanish situation, namely, the fact that what I would regard as unimpeachable testimony exists which goes to prove that there was a well-planned, long-prepared, deliberate and frightfully significant effort made by the predominant forces controlling the government of Spain, prior to Franco's counter-revolution, utterly and finally to destroy the Catholic religion in Spain— to wipe out its sacred ministry, its consecrated teachers, and its lay leaders, and in fact to "liquidate," if possible, the entire body of believers; and, thereafter, the plan was designed to proceed against the Church on all fronts, and in all the highly effective ways taught and practised by the anti-God experts of Russia, and followed, more or less successfully, more or less radically, but always in that general direction, by other atheistic revolutionary governments and parties throughout the world.

I agree with the *Commonweal's* statement that on a great many problems and situations connected with the Spanish Civil War "the information available is so generally characterized by propaganda that we do not have any sufficient knowledge" concerning them. For example, we do not precisely know to what extent the conflicting armies in Spain have or have not deliberately bombed open towns, or non-combatants, hospitals, Red Cross units, etc., as differing from the deaths and destruction caused incidentally to the prosecution of military objectives. We do not know all the facts concerning foreign assistance; we do not and cannot precisely ascertain the full truth about internal dissensions in either camp; and at best can only guess at what conditions are to be in the future if Franco wins, or if Franco loses.

But I do not see how this uncertainty can attach to our judgment concerning the war on the Catholic religion initiated by forces integrally connected with the United Front government, and uncontrolled or uncontrollable by the less violent elements connected with that government. On this matter, we have what I certainly regard as definite, objective testimony, offered to the whole world by a body of men whose sacred responsibility was higher than that of any other group of Spanish leaders, namely, the joint letter of the bishops of Spain. Incidentally, what they said was, and since its issuance has continued to be, supported by a great mass of independent testimony to the same general effect, and the records of history remain to underline its thesis with the verified accounts of the martyrdom undergone by thousands of clergymen, bishops and priests, and of nuns, and of the laity.

I am only one of those American Catholics, therefore, who cannot agree with the *Commonweal's* statement that "we are going to be forced to choose between fascism and communism," if we take sides, so far as our convictions and sympathies are concerned, in the controversies concerning the Spanish Civil War, unless we maintain "that 'positive impartiality,' a sanity of judgment toward both sides." It does not seem to us that all that is called for is simply "to express a preference for specific ideas and actions when they are certainly known." I am not, and I am fully satisfied that the overwhelming majority of American Catholics are not, and have no desire to be, either Fascist or Nazi, still less, of course, do we lean toward Communism; and I for one cannot agree that I lean toward any form of totalitarian political tyranny if I decide, and say, after reading what the Spanish bishops tell the whole world, that it is true that an anti-God revolution was let loose by, or at

least could not be stopped by, the United Front government of Madrid. In that revolution, other values prized by vast numbers of the Spanish people were also attacked. Also it is true that the United Front government, and all the parties attached to it, professed (in many cases no doubt quite sincerely) to be aiming at social justice. And I consider that the facts, not mere propaganda, show that against that revolution, with its mixed motives, but predominantly a terrorism aimed at the Catholic Church in Spain, there was a counter-revolution, led by Franco, and validated by the adhesion of a vast number, probably the majority, of the Spanish people. The dreadful disaster of civil war ensued.

It is true, no doubt, that if a universal, spontaneous desire had seized the souls of all the Spanish Catholics to submit to their own violent deaths, often by torture, and the utter destruction of all that was sacred to them and to their forefathers down the ages, rather than to resist, that such a demonstration of Christian resignation would have been, to all pacifists (and I do not write the word in sarcasm: for the truly consistent pacifist is indeed heroic) a marvellous phenomenon, infinitely preferable to any form of war—but while it is perfectly true that many of the Catholic victims of the terror went to their death peaceably, and blessing their destroyers, such exalted development of sanctity had not been achieved by the great majority of the Spaniards who followed Franco. They fought with the sword, and many, too, have perished by the sword; but even if the absolute Christian pacifists in Spain, supposing there to have been any, had exerted themselves to the utmost, they would not, it seems to me, have prevailed. The ordinary, average, humanly normal Spaniard, by hundreds of thousands, joined the Franco counter-revolution, acting as Spanish citizens, and as all citizens everywhere act, when the revolution of Communism, or Anarchism, or both combined, as in Spain, rises up against them and all that they hold dear.

TWO LETTERS TO THE NEW YORK *TIMES*

At the time of the Japanese seizure of Manchuria (1931), Henry L. Stimson, then President Hoover's Secretary of State, put forth the "Stimson Doctrine" of diplomatic nonrecognition. In January of 1939, as General Franco's armies approached Barcelona, Stimson wrote to the New York Times *and urged repeal of the embargo. His arguments were quickly challenged by Martin Conboy, a New York lawyer and Catholic layman.*

To the Editor of the New York *Times:*

I have been asked for my views concerning the present situation in Spain and the duties of our own Government and people toward that situation. The basic reasons which govern my views consist of simple and long-standing principles of American international conduct. They do not in the least depend upon ideological considerations which may or may not be involved in the conflict. On the contrary, they depend solely on the interest of our own country toward that conflict and its possible results.

First. The republican government of Spain (commonly termed the Loyalist Government) has been recognized as the true Government of Spain by our Government. The same decision has been reached by Great Britain, France, and a number of other countries. The principles upon which our Government acts in making such a decision have been well understood since the beginning of our history. They do not depend in any degree upon the internal structure of the government recognized or the domestic theories which control its relations to its citizens, whether they be Communist, Fascist, monarchial, or democratic.

Such ideological internal relations are exclusively a domestic matter for Spain itself, into which foreign governments should not intrude. That is a fundamental rule of international relations. Thomas Jefferson expressed it well as long ago as 1792:

"We certainly cannot deny to other nations that principle whereon our own Government is founded, that every nation has a right to govern itself internally under whatever forms it pleases and to change these forms at its own will; and externally to transact business with other nations through whatever organ it chooses, whether that be a king, convention, assembly, committee, president, or whatever it may be." (Jefferson to Pinckney, *Works,* vol. III, p. 500.)

When our Government several years ago through our President determined that the Spanish Government in question had control of the administrative machinery of the state with the general acquiescence of its people and was able and willing to discharge international and conventional obligations, that Spanish Government became to us and all our citizens the true Government of Spain for the purpose of our respective international relations. By this decision we admitted it as a member of the family of nations which we recognized as our friendly neighbors in the world and vested it with all of the conventional rights and privileges which we accord to such friendly neighbors.

Second. One of the most important of these rights which a state like Spain is entitled to expect from another government, which has recognized it as a friendly neighbor in the family of nations, is the right of self-defense against any future rebellions which may challenge its authority. History shows that almost every state, including our own, sooner or later in its history has to meet with the hazards of domestic strife within its borders, including an armed rebellion against its authority. In such a case the duty which the neighbor states owe to the member of the family whose authority has been challenged is perfectly well-settled. It is that such a nation has the exclusive right to the friendly assistance of its neighbors by being permitted to purchase in their markets the necessary supplies and munitions for the purpose of putting down the rebellion: and, further, that no similar assistance shall be given to the rebels who have challenged its authority. Any such assistance to the rebels would be deemed a most unfriendly act—even a cause of war— against the mother state.

Third. No nation has gone further than the United States in sustaining this general right of a nation against which civil strife or rebellion has broken out. During our own great Civil War our Federal Government insisted that it alone has the right to purchase war materials in the world at large and made vitally needed purchases of war materials abroad.

"Had England undertaken to embargo arms to both the North and the South, the North might have lost the war." (Borchard, *Neutrality for the United States,* p. 337.)

In the case of rebellions among its neighbor states the United States has acted upon the same principle and has not only given assistance to their governments but has refrained itself from giving and has prevented its nationals from giving aid to the rebels. By the joint resolution of 1912, applying to this hemisphere and somewhat more widely extended in 1922, our President has been authorized to levy embargoes against supplying arms or munitions to rebels against the authority of friendly states. To mention only a few cases, such embargoes have been levied by our Government in the case of rebellions against Cuba in 1912, Mexico in 1912, 1923, and 1929, Nicaragua in 1921, and Brazil in 1930. In these and other cases we have recognized it as our duty to assist the government and to prevent assistance from our markets reaching rebels against that government.

Furthermore, in 1928 we executed and in 1930 ratified a general convention promulgated by the Sixth Pan American Conference betwe███ ██he American republics and coverin███ ██erally this subject of the mutual rights and duties of states in the event of civil strife. This convention provided: "Article 1. The contracting states bind themselves to observe the following rules with regard to civil strife in another one of them. . . .

❋ ❋ ❋

"3. To forbid the traffic in arms and war material, except when intended for the government, while the belligerency of the rebels has not been recognized, in which latter case the rules of neutrality shall be applied."

This treaty made the previously existing traditional practice a binding rule of conduct among its signatories.

Fourth. During the Great War Secretary of State Lansing took occasion to point out why the United States was so insistent on maintaining this right of a government to buy arms and munitions in the markets of the world, whether in cases of domestic strife or of general war. As he pointed out, it was because our Nation, being a peaceful and generally unarmed nation, would have found any other rule of law most dangerous to its own safety.

"Secretary Lansing declared that the United States had from the foundation of the Republic . . . advocated and practiced unrestricted trade in arms and military supplies, because it had never been the policy of the Nation to maintain in time of peace a large military establishment or stores of arms and ammunition sufficient to repel invasion by a well-equipped and powerful enemy, and that in consequence the United States would, in the event of attack by a foreign power, be . . . seriously, if not fatally, embarrassed by the lack of arms and ammunition. . . . 'The United States has always' Lansing said, 'depended upon the right and power to purchase arms from neutral nations in case of foreign attack. This right which it claims for itself, it cannot deny to others.' He contended that a nation whose policy and principle it was to rely upon international obligations and international justice to preserve its political and territorial integrity might become the prey of an aggressive nation whose policy and practice it was to increase its military strength during times of peace

with the design of conquest, unless the nation attacked could . . . go into the markets of the world and purchase the means to defend itself against the aggressor." (Hyde, *International Law Chiefly as Interpreted and Applied by the United States,* vol. 2, at p. 752.)

Fifth. Thus under the rules of international law governing cases of insurrection against a government whose status has been recognized by its neighbors, the government itself is the only party which will be permitted to purchase arms and ammunition abroad, and any assistance to the rebels would be a violation of such international law, an unfriendly act against their government. Until the insurrection has progressed so far and successfully that a state of belligerency is recognized by the outside nations, no rules of neutrality apply. The only party recognized as lawful is the mother government at which the insurrection is aimed. In the case of Spain no such belligerency has been recognized by us or by Great Britain or by France. Under such circumstances any attempt to treat the situation as embodying the duty of neutrality is based upon a complete misconception of the rules of international law. Prof. Edwin Borchard, in his study on *Neutrality and Civil Wars, Thirty-first American Journal of Law,* at pages 304 and 305, has thus expressed the situation:

"International law requires the United States to treat the elected government of Spain as the lawful government of Spain, and, until the belligerency of the rebels is recognized, as the only government entitled to receive the assistance of the United States in suppressing armed opposition. . . . This embargo against Spain was thought to be neutrality legislation, but it seems more likely the precise opposite."

Sixth. The foregoing was the well-established practice of the world governing rebellions which occurred in the family of nations, when on July 19, 1936, the present revolt in Spain broke out against the republican government which we had recognized. Instead of following the rules of law which had theretofore been established with practical unanimity, a series of novel experiments were attempted on both sides of the Atlantic. These have resulted in a complete reversal of the pre-existing law and practice.

In Europe the conflict in Spain excited apprehension for fear that other nations might either be dragged in or voluntarily come in to fish in troubled waters. The totalitarian states, both Fascist and Communist, were apprehended to be aggressive and likely to intervene. In fact, rumor attributed to them a share in the instigation of the Franco revolt. Accordingly, in September, 1936, under the leadership of Great Britain, a special agreement of nonintervention was engineered among the neighboring nations to Spain in the hope that the conflict might be localized and the danger of its spread prevented. The first thing to be said about this agreement was that it was a complete abandonment of a code of practice which the international world had adopted through preceding ages as the best hope of achieving the same purpose and minimizing the spread of disorder. International law is the product of the efforts and experience of the nations aimed to promote peace and stability.

In the second place, however well-intentioned it may have been, an experiment based upon the promises of the totalitarian states was more wishful than sensible. Those states had already progressed too far along the primrose path of treaty violation, and the nonintervention agreement at once became a mockery and a failure. The only nations which have observed the nonintervention agreement have been the ones from whom the danger of nonintervention was not apprehended—Great Britain and France. Italy and Germany, while ostensibly accepting the obligations of the covenant, have continuously and flagrantly violated it. At the present moment, Italy is openly avowing its effective participation on the side of Franco. She is openly pushing every effort to bring the strife to a conclusion in favor of the rebels.

Thus the nonintervention agreement has simply resulted in closing to the recognized government of Spain those world markets for supplies and munitions which under the law of nations she had a right to depend upon and to have open to her purchases. It has not prevented supplies from going to the rebels who, under international law, have no right to them. Not only have the rebels been receiving arms and munitions but, as everybody now knows, they have actually received organized Italian troops in large quantities conducting for them a very large share of the fighting.

Seventh. On our side of the Atlantic there has been even less excuse for a departure from law, for we have been far remote and our interests were very unlikely to be seriously affected by the war in Spain. If we had continued our former practice and permitted the Government of Spain to make purchases in this country of arms and munitions, as we had done in the many cases which I have cited, there was no real danger that those purchases would have aroused any resentment against us from which we need have any apprehension. As a matter of fact, our Government has continued under our silver purchase law to make large purchases of Spanish silver from the

Spanish Government which undoubtedly have assisted that Government in its conduct of the war. Such purchases have not even attracted attention in the press, let alone aroused hostile acrimony against us.

In any event, we should have been following the law and could have given critics a perfectly good reason for our action. To assert that such a course of self-respecting adherence on our part to a historic policy of international law could have dragged us into war in Europe does not speak well for the balanced judgment of those who make the assertion.

But our Congress, not altogether unnaturally, may have been influenced by a desire to support the objectives of the nonintervention agreement which had just been entered into in Europe, and at that time Congress may not have foreseen that this agreement would not be faithfully observed. Congress may not have foreseen that instead of becoming a means of equal treatment toward both sides of the combatants in Spain, it would become an engine of glaring favoritism toward one side alone—the Rebels—and that the legitimate Spanish Government which by law was the only side entitled to buy arms would eventually become the only side which was unable to buy arms. At all events our Congress in January, 1937, passed a temporary resolution applying an embargo to the sale of arms to both the combatants in Spain. And on May 1, 1937, this temporary resolution was superseded by Public Resolution No. 27. By the language of that resolution the exportation of munitions to any foreign State was prohibited on a proclamation by the President that "a state of civil strife exists . . . and that such civil strife is of a magnitude or is being conducted under such conditions that the export of arms . . . would . . . endanger the peace

of the United States." On the same day, May 1, 1937, the President imposed the present embargo against Spain.

Eighth. The results have shown how futile as well as dangerous novel experiments in international law can be. The United States on its part has abandoned a traditional policy to which for a century and a half it had carefully adhered as a means of protecting the peace and stability of nations, which like itself, preferred to live not armed to the teeth. It is likely to sorely rue the day when that principle was abandoned and when it consented to a new precedent which may hereafter weight the scale in favor of a militaristic and thoroughly armed nation.

On the other hand; the progress of events during the past 2 years in Spain has served to demonstrate the vitality of the Loyalist Government and thus has tended to confirm the correctness of our Government's decision when we recognized that Loyalist Government as representative of the people of Spain.

To an extent which probably few anticipated, that Loyalist Government has succeeded in defending itself not only against a surprise attack by its own rebellious army, but against a powerful combination of aggressive interveners by land and sea and air. By so doing it has furnished strong evidence of its vitality and of the fact that it must be supported by the great mass of the people within its territory. Starting without an army of its own, forced to organize and train its raw militia, conspicuously lacking in the powerful modern guns, planes, and other munitions which have been available to its opponents, it has for many months been putting up a most surprising and gallant defense against opponents who have had every advantage in the way of land and naval organization and who are illegally aided both on land and on sea by powerful organized forces from Italy and Germany.

If this Loyalist Government is overthrown, it is evident now that its defeat will be solely due to the fact that it has been deprived of its right to buy from us and other friendly nations the munitions necessary for its defense. I cannot believe that our Government or our country would wish to assume such a responsibility.

Ninth. In short, I have come to the conclusion that the embargo imposed under the resolution of May 1, 1937, should be at once lifted by the President. By its terms I believe he has the power to take such action. The change in the international situation during the past 2 years would justify such action by him. The embargo, which by the terms of the law authorizing it was intended as a protection against conditions which would endanger the peace of the United States, is now shown by the events of the past 2 years to be itself a source of danger to that peace. Any danger that may come to the people of the United States from the situation in Spain would arise not from any lawful sale of munitions in our markets to the Government of Spain, but from the assistance which our embargo has given to the enemies of Spain. It is the success of the lawless precedents created by those enemies which would constitute our real danger. There is no reason why we should ourselves facilitate and accentuate that danger. There is still less reason why we should violate our own historic policy to do so. The prestige and safety of our country will not be promoted by abandoning its self-respecting traditions in order to avoid the hostility of reckless violators of international law in Europe.

Henry L. Stimson

New York, January 23, 1939.

To the Editor of the New York *Times:*

In his letter to the New York *Times* published in your issue of today Mr. Henry L. Stimson presents his views "concerning the present situation in Spain and the duties of our own Government and people toward that situation." He adds that "the basic reasons which govern my views consist of simple and long-standing principles of American international conduct," and he advocates the lifting of the embargo on arms to Spain by Presidential proclamation. My own view of the matter differs in that I consider the American reason for keeping the Spanish embargo is that it conforms to our national neutrality policy, and further, that, irrespective of whether it should or should not be maintained, the embargo can only be removed by the repeal by Congress of a joint resolution of Congress adopted on January 8, 1937.

The neutrality policy of this country was established when the United States were formed as a separate nation. The policy was declared by the first President of the United States. It was enacted in one of the first laws adopted by the Congress of the United States. The policy has never been narrowed. Whenever there have been any modifications of it they have all been by way of enlargement to make it more effective.

The policy has been extended to include the prohibition of the sale of arms and munitions of war. Coming to recent instances, the neutrality law, passed August 31, 1935, made the export of arms, ammunition, and implements of war from the United States to any belligerent state unlawful whenever the President found that there existed a state of war between two foreign states. Within a month after this enactment the Italian attack on Ethiopia began. On October 5, 1935, President Roosevelt issued two proclamations, one forbidding shipment of munitions to the belligerents, the other giving notice that American citizens could travel on belligerent ships only at their own risk.

When civil war broke out in Spain, July, 1936, the President had no authority to lay an embargo on the exportation of munitions and implements of war to Spain for the use of either side, because the then existing neutrality legislation did not apply to a condition of civil war.

Nevertheless, the established policy of the United States was opposed to such traffic and, accordingly, on August 7, 1936, the Assistant Secretary of State informed all American consular representatives in Spain that "in conformity with its well-established policy of noninterference with internal affairs in other countries, either in time of peace or in the event of civil strife, this Government will, of course, scrupulously refrain from any interference whatsoever in the unfortunate Spanish situation." No licenses were issued by the Federal Munitions Control Board and none, in fact, was sought, until December, 1936. Then an American company applied for a license to export airplanes and engines to the Loyalist Government of Spain. The Board, which had refused licenses for the exportation of arms and munitions to Italy and Ethiopia during the war between those countries, was without authority in law to refuse licenses to ship such articles to Spain.

The editor of the *British Year Book of International Law*, 1937, commenting upon this situation, says:

"With evident regret, therefore, the board felt obliged to issue the licenses in the present case, and it did so. The President publicly expressed his disapproval of the action of the Cuse Co. in refusing to comply with the Government's nonin-

tervention policy, although he admitted that the company was within its legal rights in shipping the airplanes and engines to the Spanish Government. At the same time he caused the various governments of Europe most directly concerned to be informed of his sincere regrets and of the intention of the Government of the United States to continue to pursue a policy of strict neutrality in the present civil war."

The President publicly characterized as "unpatriotic" such shipments as had been made and deprecated "the unfortunate noncompliance by an American citizen with this Government's strict nonintervention policy."

Thereupon, on January 8, 1937, Congress passed a joint resolution. This is a special act to stop the exportation of arms and munitions to Spain. It is founded on the well-established policy of the United States which had been violated by the shipments made before there was any statute prohibiting them. It reads—

"That during the existence of the state of civil strife now obtaining in Spain it shall from and after the approval of this resolution, be unlawful to export arms, ammunition, or implements of war from any place in the United States to Spain or to any other foreign country for transshipment to Spain or for use of either of the opposing forces in Spain."

The embargo specifically laid by this resolution can be lifted only upon proclamation by the President that the state of war has ceased to exist.

The next step in the expression by Congress of our well-established principle of neutrality was the writing into our neutrality statute by joint resolution adopted May 1, 1937, of a general provision relating to civil strife in any foreign country. The President was thereby authorized to establish an embargo by proclamation upon a finding by him that a state of civil strife existed in such country and "that such civil strife is of a magnitude or is being conducted under such conditions that the export of arms, ammunition, or implements of war from the United States to such foreign state would threaten or endanger the peace of the United States."

Upon the same day the President, acting under the authority of that joint resolution, issued a proclamation with relation to Spain admonishing all citizens and residents of the United States to abstain from the exportation of arms, ammunition, or implements of war from any place in the United States to Spain or to any other State for transportation to or for the use of Spain under the penalties provided for in this statute. This proclamation had no effect upon the embargo existing under the joint resolution of January 8, 1937, except to permit the President to invoke certain administrative powers given him by the later resolution which had not been contained in the earlier one.

Mr. Stimson, in his letter to the *Times,* refers to the joint resolution of January 8 as a "temporary resolution," which he says "was superseded" by that of May 1. Upon that assumption he continues by saying that "the embargo imposed under the resolution of May 1, 1937, should be at once lifted by the President. By its terms I believe he has the power to take such action." But Mr. Stimson ignores the fact that the President has not the power to lift the embargo which was imposed by Congress in its joint resolution of January 8, 1937, until the state of civil strife has ceased in Spain.

Secretary of State Hull, undoubtedly with the advice of the eminent legal staff in his office, and probably also under the advice of the Department of Justice, wrote, on March 21, 1938, to the president of the Foreign Policy Association, New York, the following:

"It is manifest that the state of civil strife in Spain described in the joint resolution of Congress of January 8, 1937, has not ceased to exist. Accordingly, even if the proclamation of the President of May 1, 1937, were to be revoked (lifting the embargo under the general resolution of that date), the prohibition upon the export of arms, ammunition, and implements of war to Spain laid down in the joint resolution of Congress approved January 8, 1937, would still remain in effect."

This conclusion necessarily follows from the well-settled rule of statutory construction that when there are two statutes upon the same subject, the earlier being special and the later general, the special statute remains in force in the absence of an express repeal or absolute incompatibility.

Mr. Stimson stresses what he claims to be the duty of this country toward "the recognized Government of Spain." In his argument based thereon he ignores the purpose of our neutrality policy, which is to keep us out of European disputes. It does not make the slightest difference whether the situation is a state of war between two nations or a state of civil war, where aiding by supplying arms to either or both parties to the war will be productive of danger to our peace.

There is a condition of civil war in Spain. After 2 years of fighting, the insurgents are in control of 35 of the 50 provinces in Spain, and more than half of the population of the country is within the territory they control. Sympathy with one side or the other has no more to do with the invocation and applicability of our policy than would sympathy as between two warring nations. When two nations are involved in war it makes no difference, so far as our policy is concerned, whether we sympathize with one or the other. Our neutrality policy is to assist neither.

This is not the first time the United States has been urged to adapt its neutrality policy to the preference of some of our citizens for one or other of foreign combatants. Washington had to face exactly that difficulty. France had been on our side in the Revolution. France, at war with England afterward, presumed upon that friendship by acts inconsistent with our neutrality. And Washington refused to have our policy of neutrality so invaded.

So, likewise, when a condition of civil strife exists, our established policy of neutrality is equally applicable. The converse of neutrality is assistance to one or another of the belligerent parties. In short, the change demanded by those who favor the lifting of the present embargo under the circumstances would mean an affirmative act of aid and assistance in favor of one of the belligerent parties as against the other.

In the present instance, insistence upon maintenance of the integrity of our well-established policy of neutrality and upon the lack of power of the President to lift the embargo imposed by Congress in its resolution of January 8, 1937, need not preclude us from inquiring whether, if the matter were one of mere temporary expediency, the President was well advised in affirming that the export of arms and munitions does tend to threaten or endanger the peace of the United States.

Within limits there can be no complaint against those who hold that the cause of one of the parties to the civil strife in Spain is better than the cause of the other party. Those who are endowed with sight and hearing are aware that the minds of men and women are occupied with the relative merits of the various political cults now popular in Europe.

Where might this lead us? Congress knew by experience how easy it is for the acts of citizens to get us into a situation in which the peace of the United States would be endangered. How to avoid being led into a situation of that kind was a more difficult problem.

We had been in very much the same position 20 years before when the World War started in 1914. We know the United States had no part in the maneuvers that precipitated the declaration of war. And we know, also, that partly through what we did ourselves, and might have refrained from doing, we were drawn irresistibly into the war before it ended.

Just how and why the United States did get into the Great War has been the subject of innumerable volumes. But there were some facts concerning which Congress could not be in doubt.

We did take contracts for arms and munitions, and whether by our own choice or because the control of the seas left us no choice we did supply, without limit or restraint, arms, munitions, contraband of war, to one set of contestants. We did take pay for all this in securities of one set of belligerents. And we thereby exposed ourselves to the enmity of the other side. We had made ourselves in their eyes their potential enemies, and were exposed by our own acts to retaliation by them if the end of the war left them in position to retaliate.

When we had been drawn into the war by the inexorable logic of events and had come out of it as participants in victory, we found we were left with billions of debt. We paid, or we are still paying, a large portion of the cost of the war. What we lost in lives and in the wrecked lives of our wounded, and in the care of these latter, likewise go into the account.

We achieved nothing for ourselves, nor did we succeed in bringing peace to Europe as was evident in 1935 and is still more evident now.

Congress surely was justified in insisting that we must try to avoid like consequences of avoidable errors. They thought it well, while we could still do so without being under the influence of the passions that such a war in Europe must engender among us, even if we were not participants, to take thought about those actions of our own that could be identified as having in any considerable measure been contributory factors to our entry into that war. The legislation that resulted in 1935, amplified in 1937, undoubtedly represented the sober judgment of the American people.

We made these enactments in development of our well-established policy to safeguard the peace of the United States. We made them because we concluded, by our costly experience, that our established policy had to be extended.

We abandoned the profitable business of selling arms and munitions. We abandoned the more deceptive expectation of profits from lending money on Government securities. We put behind us the indignation aroused by loss of lives that came from traveling on ships of belligerent nations. We cut clear of all the disputes that came when a neutral nation tried to maintain its place on the sea against the action of belligerents. And we decided that the favor and profit to be drawn from belligerents benefiting by our arms, munitions, and credits was too dearly bought at the price of the threat and danger to the peace of the United States involved in such transactions.

It is true that in the neutrality legislation of 1935 and 1937 the major preoccupation of Congress was directed to the possibility of a world war. But as long ago as 1912, having in mind the supreme desirability of peace in this hemisphere, Congress provided for embargoes upon the exportation of arms or ammunition "whenever the President shall find that in any American country conditions of domestic violence exist which are promoted by the use of arms or munitions of war procured from the United States."

By an amendment of 1922 the resolution was extended to include, in addition, "any country in which the United States exercises extraterritorial jurisdiction," and the President's authority was broadened by authorizing him to include cases where conditions of domestic violence "are or may be" promoted by the use of munitions procured from the United States.

Under this law proclamations have been issued prohibiting shipments of arms to Mexico, to China, to Honduras, to Cuba, to Nicaragua, and to Brazil.

On May 28, 1934, the sale of arms and munitions of war to Paraguay and Bolivia, then engaged in armed conflict in the Chaco, was prohibited.

When these laws were adopted, the United States was not the only possible purveyor of arms and munitions. But the United States did not make its policy contingent upon adoption of the same policy by others.

Need we be surprised, therefore, that when the Spanish civil war developed, Congress expressed no concern for the fact that arms and munitions could be purchased elsewhere by one or both of the parties to the civil strife? The peace of the United States was held to be of greater importance than the competition in manufacture and sale of arms.

We are to suppose that Congress had

in mind something other than a theoretical gesture, and that the President, when he said he found a condition that would threaten and endanger the peace of the United States if we sent arms to Spain, meant just what he said.

There is no need for doubt on that point.

There were present all the elements necessary to "threaten and endanger the peace of the United States" sooner or later, and to threaten and endanger it not in relation to Spain alone but to the much more potent forces that have transformed all Europe into armed camps.

So far as the United States could go to avoid being drawn into danger by acts of its own, Congress and the President were bound to go, and the people of the United States resolutely desired them to go.

If we were to seek evidence that the precautions then taken were well-advised, we have only to recall the bare outlines of what has happened since. A Norwegian ship had been sunk in December, 1936; a French ship bombed in January, 1937; three British ships in February, and two French ships in March. The bombing of French and British ships in the harbors of Barcelona and Valencia has been a frequent feature of the news during the past 2 years.

We in the United States can be well content to have no immediate interest in such news. Nor can we limit this consideration to the civil strife in Spain as a separate entity. We must recall that week in September last when peace and war hung in the balance and when the frontier between France and Spain was plainly marked as one of the battlegrounds included in the plans of the two great rival forces that from hour to hour seemed likely to be engaged in a conflict by which European civilization would have been destroyed.

The threat of general war has not yet passed. And yet, with that danger facing us, with the prospect that the utmost exertion may be required to maintain the security of the United States in the midst of a toppling civilization, there are those who seriously and with unaccountable insistence demand that our well-established policy shall now be reversed.

It is demanded that legislation designed to keep this nation at peace shall be replaced by legislation that would lead to our again being trapped into war.

In my humble judgment, the people of the United States will have none of it.

Conditions that "would threaten and endanger the peace of the United States" are not to be lightly passed over, even if the desire of those who seek the change is to improve the chances of one of the contending elements in the Spanish strife.

Our preferences, either as to Spain or as to the world at large, may be as the poles apart, but when it comes to endangering deliberately the peace of the United States over the quarrels of other peoples, the solid good sense of the American people is certain to prevail.

Yours truly,

Martin Conboy

New York, January 24, 1939.

Joseph F. Thorning: NEUTRALITY VS. INTERVENTION

Reverend Joseph F. Thorning, teacher of history and sociology at Mount Saint Mary's College, became, during the Spanish Civil War, one of the most articulate defenders of General Franco's Movimiento Nacional. Father Thorning visited Spain, interviewed General Franco, and wrote for Spain, *an English-language magazine sponsored by the Nationalists. In the essay reprinted below, Father Thorning contributes to the debate over the last-minute campaign to lift the Spanish embargo.*

THE movement to lift the embargo on arms to Spain rests upon two false assumptions. The first is that the so-called Loyalist Government is the legal government of Spain; the second that a policy of American neutrality has worked to the disadvantage of Barcelona, although favoring the shipment of arms from Germany and Italy to Burgos. These are the two main contentions of those who are straining every nerve to repeal or modify the neutrality legislation of the United States Government.

The first claim of the Leftists is nullified by the fact that whatever shreds of legality the Republican Government may have possessed were scattered to the four winds by the brutal murder of Calvo Sotelo on July 13th, 1936. This crime was the climax of chaos, anarchy, and political assassination. During the five preceding months 256 persons had been killed, 170 churches, 69 clubs, and the offices of 10 newspapers had been set on fire. Attempts had been made to burn 284 other buildings including 251 churches. There had been 113 general strikes and 218 partial strikes.

Throughout June and during the early days of July the pages of the newspapers were filled with reports of shootings, strikes, casualties, violent scenes at funerals, riots, arson, destruction. This was the setting for the arrest and execution of Calvo Sotelo, the talented Rightist Deputy. It occasioned an emotion of horror corresponding to the shock that would be inflicted upon American public opinion were the morning newspapers to announce the slaying of Charles Evans Hughes with the connivance and help of the authorities.

"Left and Right alike," writes Professor E. Allison Peers, "were shaken at the audacity of the crime, while the man in the street, dumbfounded with horror, saw it as the climax beyond which crime could not farther go. 'This,' he said, perhaps not knowing exactly what he meant, 'must be the end.'" (*The Tragedy of Spain,* by Prof. E. Allison Peers, p. 210.)

It was the end of the Republican régime's pretensions to speak or act for the Spanish people. When a government itself becomes the chief lawbreaker, its claims to legality automatically cease. A reign of terror, culminating in gangsterdom's murderous technique, loses juridical and moral content. In the calm perspective of history there are none who try

From Rev. Fr. Joseph F. Thorning, "Neutrality versus Intervention," in *Spain,* III (February 1, 1939), pp. 5, 19, 21.

to justify the rule of Robespierre. The Spanish Republic from February to July, 1936, proved its utter incapacity for administration, exposing the Spanish citizenry to the caprice and fury of mob rule. The "law of nature and nature's God" imposed an obligation upon the decent elements of the community to reconstruct the State.

This was the origin of the Nationalist movement in Spain. To have delayed beyond July 18th, 1936, would have jeopardized the fabric of European civilization. The sole alternative to armed self-defense would have been to witness the death of other Spanish statesmen and passively to accept the Marxist yoke.

Integral to this phase of the question is the actual attitude of the Spanish people. The overwhelming majority of the Spaniards now recognize Generalissimo Francisco Franco as the head of the State. His government controls more than eighty per cent of the territory and seventy-five per cent of the population of Spain. From the standpoint of fact and reality this question is swiftly being removed from the domain of academic theory. Openly to take sides against an established, functioning régime is no part of the American tradition.

The Leftist contention that Nationalist Spain has benefited by the operation of our neutrality legislation is pure chimera. President Franklin D. Roosevelt himself is on record as stating that "neutrality works." On Friday, April 22nd, 1938, at his regular press conference the President, in response to questions, declared that he was satisfied with the manner in which the laws had been administered in the Spanish difficulties, considering the many difficulties involved.

Writers on foreign affairs, it was stated in the New York *Times* (Saturday, April 23rd, 1938), had "hoped to get the President to take cognizance of criticisms that the Neutrality Act was functioning to the detriment of the Spanish Loyalist cause because of German purchases of munitions in this country allegedly destined for delivery to the Insurgent forces."

The President made it clear, said the New York *Times* in the same dispatch, that "he wanted no unwarranted inferences drawn from his reply to a question that pertained only to Germany and Italy and their part in the Spanish conflict." Asked whether an arms embargo could be applied to these Fascist States, Mr. Roosevelt "quickly lengthened the question by asking, 'or Britain or France?' He then answered in the negative."

Obviously, the President of the United States was perfectly familiar with the fact that Soviet Russia had been shipping as much, or more material of war to Barcelona than was being supplied to the Nationalists by Germany and Italy. The records of the British Parliament are available both to the President and to the U.S. Secretary of State. It may be safely assumed that most responsible American officials were and are familiar with the significant declaration of Captain Anthony Eden, at that time Foreign Secretary of Great Britain (October 31st, 1937), to the following effect:

Official Soviet Government figures show that Spain now is Soviet Russia's best customer. From January to September of this year Russia shipped to Spain nearly ten times as much in weight and four and one-half times as much in value as during the corresponding period in 1936. During the summer months of this year I could not stand at this box and tell the House that during that period there was more material reaching the Insurgent forces than was reaching the Government forces.

On the same day in the House of Commons (Cf. the New York *Times*, November 1st, 1937), in refuting David Lloyd George, Foreign Secretary Eden

summed up the results of the non-intervention agreement as follows:

The result of Nyon has been to facilitate
the arrival of very large quantities of material arriving in Spanish Government ports.
Of course there have been enormous quantities of material arriving at Spanish Government ports throughout the year.

Similar testimony, even more convinc-
ingly presented, is given by Sir Francis
Lindley, G.C.M.G., C.B., former British
Ambassador to Japan. In an article, "The
Tragedy of Spain," published in the *National Review* (February, 1937), Sir Francis traces the origin of Soviet intervention to its ideology of exploiting every
"revolutionary situation." The British
diplomat declares: "The plain fact is
clear to all who wish to see. The Spanish
civil war would have been a purely internal affair had it not been for Moscow.
No other Power would have had either
reason or wish to intervene. Once the
Bolsheviks set the example, others were
certain to come in on the opposite side."

Edward H. Knoblaugh of the Associated Press, who was in an excellent position to judge, assures us (*Correspondent
in Spain,* p. 174) that "the foreign assistance Loyalist Spain was receiving was
successfully minimized while that given
the enemy assumed staggering proportions." The same writer estimated that
the Madrid-Valencia-Barcelona Government has about 110,000 Russian, French,
German, Italian, American, Polish, English, Czech, and Bulgarian volunteers
fighting on its side. Of these, about 35,000
were killed, leaving some 75,000 still fit
for service (*Correspondent in Spain,* Edward H. Knoblaugh, p. 217). This esti-
mate is confirmed by Brig.-Gen. P. R. C.
Grove of the *Observer* (London).

Largely through the instrumentality of
the Communist Party and Communistic
affiliates six thousand American boys

were sent to Leftist Spain. The recruiting
for this force properly should be a subject of investigation by some appropriate
committee of the United States Congress.
Why should 2,000 Americans fight and
die in a foreign war? This illegal recruiting and illegal entrance of Americans
into Spain during the Civil War shows
clearly enough the respect for national
and passport regulations entertained by
pro-Loyalist Communistic elements in
the United States. Arms were illegally
shipped to the Spanish Ambassador in
Mexico; airplanes were dispatched to the
same destination; monies were collected
to support mercenaries in a foreign conflict. Every breach of American laws in
respect to the Spanish war was perpetrated by the Loyalist sympathizers.
Nothing of the kind was imputed to those
who favored and still favor neutrality.
The contrast in the attitude and activities
of the two groups is an index to their
patriotic spirit. Nevertheless, the Loyalists, who cannot come into court with
clean hands, are pleading for partisan action on the part of the nation, whose laws
were violated.

How lavishly the French and Russians
poured ammunition into Leftist Spain
last spring may be learned from the special dispatch of Mr. George Axelsson,
whose story was featured on page one of
the New York *Times* on April 13th, 1938.
This highly circumstantial report by an
eyewitness reads as follows:

At the French frontier town of Le Perthus,
on the main motor road to Barcelona, this
writer has watched for many days a seemingly endless stream of ten-ton trucks cross-
ing into Spain. A customs official told me
the daily average was 200 trucks, which
the simplest arithmetic will show means
2,000 tons of material entering Loyalist
Spain every day. Another customs employee
confided to me that he had personally passed
a score of airplanes and a dozen whippet

tanks into Spain during the past week. They were listed on manifests as "agricultural machinery" and passed as such, he explained.

This traffic was carried on at enormous expense to the Leftist Government, which naturally enough is now forced to beg for food from other countries. The gold that should have been husbanded for the necessities of life for the civilian population was squandered upon war supplies that prolonged the war futilely, foolishly. An interesting sidelight upon this phase of the question is afforded by Mr. George Axelsson's further description. He says:

A great deal of these materials originate at Marseilles, Le Havre and other ports, whence they are trucked across France. The trucks as well as the drivers are all French. Army drivers, specially selected for their daring, are stationed at Le Perthus and are taking these cargoes south for double pay. As a result this normally quiet border spot has become a truck drivers' Klondike where, relaxing after risky trips, the men indulge in champagne and such culinary niceties as snails, frogs legs, asparagus and speckled trout.

In other words, the civil populations of Madrid, Valencia, and Barcelona are now starving because the $650,000,000 gold reserve, the property of the whole nation, has been wasted in riotous living for the arms racketeers, gun-runners, Russian and French "merchants of death."

Further confirmation of this view is contained in the Washington dispatch of Mr. Hanson W. Baldwin, famous arms expert of the New York *Times* (April 13th, 1938). Mr. Baldwin writes:

The "last-ditch" defense of the Spanish Loyalists has been unexpectedly bolstered by the receipt of a considerable number of planes and some artillery from abroad, it was learned here today.

Neither the amount nor the make of the equipment was known, but it was presumed that both the planes and the artillery were of Russian manufacture or design.

This latest foreign intervention in Spain, unexpected and surprising in view of the apparently desperate plight of the government armies, was not believed to be extensive enough to change the complexion of the struggle or even halt the drive for the sea which the Insurgent forces started in Northeastern Spain on March 9th.

Despite the receipt of new equipment, it is not believed, however, that the hard-pressed government forces can long resist the Franco drive, unless reinforced very extensively by outside aid.

Mr. Baldwin's prognosis has been found correct. One year ago, the Leftists reported a smashing victory at Teruel. Propagandists in this country, such as Mr. Jay Allen, who visited the battlefront, declared categorically that Teruel was "a huge, a tremendous, a decisive victory." Within four weeks of this triumphant communiqué the Leftists were in full retreat, a retreat that soon assumed the proportions of a flight. Last summer, the Loyalists initiated another offensive. Gandesa was reported to be the objective. Gandesa remained in the power of the Nationalists, whereas the Leftists were thrown back across the Ebro River. This was the first blow to the present Nationalist thrust that has embraced more than half of Catalonia.

In spite of huge war supplies from Soviet Russia the Barcelona régime is *in articulo mortis*. Barring a world war or American intervention, the struggle will be concluded before the summer. As Brig. Gen. Henry Joseph Reilly, U.S.A., declares, "no army can be beaten day after day and remain in the field." The Loyalist cause, which is the Communist cause throughout the world, is a "lost cause." The frontic [sic] efforts of the Left-wingers to stir up trouble, to incite hatred, to embroil the United States are merely another illustration of the desperate character of their predicament. They know that they are playing their last card in trying to enlist the U.S. Government on the side of the persecutors and would-be destroyers of Christianity in Spain. The motto of clear-sighted, democratic, liberty-loving citizens everywhere is crystallized in these words: KEEP THE EMBARGO ON ARMS; KEEP THIS COUNTRY OUT OF WAR!

From The New Republic: A TELEGRAM TO THE PRESIDENT

> *Since 1914, the* New Republic *has championed liberal or socialist causes, but none more ardently than the cause of the Spanish Republic. As the embargo controversy intensified to feverish heat, the editors begged President Roosevelt to lift the embargo.*

President Roosevelt, the White House, Washington:

A few days ago Father Coughlin spoke against raising the Spanish embargo, because of his favor for the cause of the Fascist Franco. At the same time a number of Catholic authorities from their pulpits urged their ill-informed flocks to bring pressure to bear on Washington to the same end. As a result telegrams and letters went to you, to Senators and Representatives by the hundred thousand. Believers in progressive democracy are not so well disciplined and are not so accustomed to making peremptory demands; nevertheless it is well for those who disagree with the reactionaries among the Catholics to make their position known. This editorial is therefore being sent to you by wire; its burden is to urge you to act at once in raising the unneutral embargo which is helping to turn Spain over to the friend of Hitler and Mussolini.

You surely cannot be deceived by the Coughlin-sponsored telegrams. The Gallup poll, the accuracy of which you have good reason to know, recently sounded American public opinion on this question. It showed that two-thirds of the people had chosen sides in the Spanish civil war, and that of those who had chosen, 76 percent favored the Loyalists and only 24 percent the Rebels. Even American Catholics, in spite of the announced preference of the Pope and the intensive propaganda of other Church authorities, voted only about 40 percent for Franco. We do not suppose you would be intimidated, in executing a policy in which you believed, by the prospect of losing votes— but in this case there is not even a danger of following an unpopular course if you should act.

Why do you not act, and act at once? Why did you not act long ago? We confess that your policy in this matter is a tragic mystery to us.

Nobody has more forcefully than you denounced the aggressors and enemies of democracy in the present world. Nobody has more often expressed a desire not to aid these aggressors. Do you not know that Spain is now a battlefield where the aggressors and the enemies of democracy are fighting to stamp out the last vestiges of liberalism? Do you not know that the so-called "non-interven-

From "A Telegram to the President," *The New Republic*, XCVII (February 1, 1939), p. 357.

tion" policy, under which we refuse to permit shipment of arms to either side, is a cloak under which Hitler and Mussolini have long been arming Franco to the teeth, while the constitutional Spanish government is starved of assistance from the democratic powers?

Nobody has striven more earnestly than you to save Latin America for democracy. Do you not know that the biggest single influence in this struggle is that of Spanish institutions and culture, and that a victory for Franco would be a stunning defeat for your policy?

Do you blame the Neutrality Act, of which you disapprove, for the existence of the embargo? The *New Republic* approves of this act in the main, yet it has never approved of the Spanish embargo. The principal authors of the Act wanted to change the policy of this nation toward Spain months ago, and undoubtedly would have obtained a majority in Congress for doing so, but your Department of State prevented them. Do you not know that the embargo was imposed, not by the Neutrality Act, but by a special resolution passed by Congress at your urgent request, and applying only to Spain? Do you not know that the subsequent Neutrality Act makes your power to impose embargoes discretionary in the case of civil wars? Do you not know that so great an authority as ex-Secretary of State Henry L. Stimson believes that the act supersedes the resolution, and that without any further authorization from Congress you can lift the embargo?

Perhaps you are advised that Mr. Stimson is wrong about this. But if so, why have you never asked, and why do you not now ask, Congress for the power to permit the sale of arms to Spain, at least on the cash-and-carry basis? Do you think that might embroil us in a European war? We, who favor the Neu-

trality Act because we believe it would be unwise to sell arms in a general European war, do not think so, and never have. Neither Germany nor Italy could or would challenge us forcibly for allowing munitions to be shipped to Spain. Why should you, who want to amend the main provisions of the act and place embargoes only on aggressors even in a general war, be so hesitant?

Is the course of this country determined by the wishes of Prime Minister Chamberlain of Great Britain, the chief and stubborn supporter of the cynical "non-intervention" policy? If so, why? Since when have British Tories acted as a guide for progressive Americans? Do you not know that, at least in this instance, Chamberlain is as great an enemy of our interests as Hitler and Mussolini?

Franco is now at the gates of Barcelona. Perhaps you believe that it is too late to do anything. But you probably believed that last spring, when Franco was making his drive to the sea. Yet it was not too late; if you had acted then, the course of world history might have been different. The Spanish democratic forces are not ready to surrender; they have resolved to resist as long as any possibility of resistance remains. Disaster may be imminent, but we should not accept it until we are forced to do so. If you act today, this hour, you might turn the tide in France, in England, even in Spain!

Mr. President, we urge you not to hesitate or delay. We can imagine no valid reason for you to do so. You have spoken bravely—in some cases, we believe, so bravely as to be foolhardy. But here is something that you can safely do —and do now. Why not make your acts correspond with your words?

The Editors of the *New Republic*

III. NEUTRALITY IN RETROSPECT

Allen Guttmann: AN INDICTMENT OF AMERICAN POLICY

> *Despite such plans as that of the* New Republic, *President Roosevelt maintained the embargo until the end of the war. The Loyalist forces began to collapse after the fall of Barcelona and finally surrendered at the end of March, 1939. General Franco announced final victory on April 1, 1939, and received American diplomatic recognition on that day.*
>
> *The debate, however, continues. When the problem of American neutrality and the Spanish Civil War was first raised as a problem for Amherst College's course in American Civilization, Allen Guttmann and John G. Gagliardo differed vehemently on the wisdom of American policy. The concluding selections are based upon their lectures.*

ON December 7, 1941, the Japanese bombed Pearl Harbor. President Franklin Roosevelt characterized that day as one which will live in the annals of infamy. On December 8th, he asked Congress for a declaration of war. Congress complied. But the President and the Congress were five years too late. The first Americans to fight in World War II had long since embarked. They had sailed from New York on the *Normandie,* on December 26, 1936, and they had gone into battle on February 23, 1937, on the Jarama Front, south of Madrid. They formed part of the XVth International Brigade, and they fought for the Spanish Republic. There were 428 of them on February 23rd. 127 were killed in the first attack; 200 more were wounded. These were the first American casualties of World War II.

These men risked their citizenship as well as their lives, for the Department of State had announced that Americans may not take oaths of allegiance to foreign governments and that enlistment in the Spanish army was "unpatriotically inconsistent with the American Government's policy of the most scrupulous nonintervention in the Spanish internal affairs." My argument today is that the men who fought in the Lincoln Battalion were right and that Cordell Hull and Franklin Roosevelt were wrong. The ban on volunteers was wrong and the embargo of January 8, 1937, was catastrophically wrong. Pearl Harbor was the price Franklin Roosevelt paid for his shortsightedness.

I want at the outset to be clear about one thing: the embargo of January 8, 1937, did not injure the *Movimiento Nacional* of General Franco. It *did* injure the Spanish Republic. No one at the time was confused about this. Only the most hypocritical could pretend, after the spring of 1937, that the embargo was impartial. Nazi Germany and Fascist Italy poured men and equipment into Spain and quickly abandoned even the pretense of non-intervention. Although the Soviet Union sent equipment and approximately 500 men to the Republic, Germany and Italy were in a far better position geographically and militarily. Not only was it easier to ship supplies from Hamburg or Naples to Cádiz or Málaga, it was a simple matter for Italian submarines to torpedo ships bound for Republican Spain. And I assure you that ships were—contrary to whole volumes of international law—bombed or torpedoed. The alleged impartiality of the embargo was like the impartiality of the famous French law on bridges: neither the rich nor the poor were allowed to sleep under the bridges of Paris; similarly, the Republic could not buy the arms it needed, and the Nationalists could not buy the arms they did not need.

No one at the time was confused about this. Americans who were *for* General Franco were unanimously in favor of retention of the embargo. Americans who were *against* General Franco were divided. Some felt that the Republic ought to be sacrificed to the greater good of American neutrality. Others felt that the embargo ought to be raised so that a friendly Republic could survive. No one who sympathized with the Republic thought that the embargo worked to the Republic's advantage.

My next question is this: was American public opinion pro-Loyalist or pro-Nationalist? If most Americans *wanted* General Franco to win, the embargo was a useful instrument for attaining the will of the majority. If, on the other hand, most Americans wanted the Republic to survive, then the embargo acted to thwart the will of the majority.

It is always difficult to know what The People want, but public opinion polls—despite their inaccuracies—are a help. Four Gallup Polls dealt with the Spanish Civil War. The first was published on January 11, 1937—almost immediately after the embargo. Americans were, on the whole, for the Republic by a ratio of 2-to-1. The poll is broken into occupa-

tional categories—professional men, businessmen, etc., into geographical categories—New England, the South, etc., and into political categories—Republican, Democrat. In every category, Loyalist sympathy prevailed. In the professional category—doctors, lawyers, teachers, etc. —the partisans of the Republic outnumbered those of General Franco by 3-to-1. Only in the category of the "Unemployed" did the percent of Nationalist sympathy creep to within three points of the percent of Republican sympathy. As the war continued, the split was widened. Americans came increasingly to support the Republic and decreasingly to support General Franco. By February 3, 1938, the pro-Loyalist ratio was up to 3-to-1. Only 17 percent of those who gave an opinion were in favor of General Franco. By the end of the year, this group had shrunk to 14 percent of those who gave an opinion. In each poll, the highest percentage of Loyalist support came from professional people and the highest percentage of Nationalist support came from the unemployed. And, even among the unskilled workers and the unemployed, twice as many Americans were for the Republic as were for General Franco.

If we leave the polls and examine the statements of individual Americans or of groups of Americans, we find that pro-Loyalist sympathy was much more intense among the articulate than among those who responded only when hunted down by the indefatigable Gallup. Consider writers. The League of American Writers gathered the responses to a questionnaire of 418 American writers. They included almost every writer of any importance whatsoever. Only seven writers remained neutral. Only one was for the Nationalists. Consider another group whom we rightly consider among the more educated and enlightened, college presidents. Rather than quote from all the college presidents who were for the Republic, from ex-President Meiklejohn of Amherst through the alphabet to the president of Yale, I'll read the names of the college presidents who signed one single petition urging that the embargo be raised: Samuel B. Capen of the University of Buffalo, Robert B. Clothier of Rutgers, Ada L. Comstock of Radcliffe, Frank Graham of the University of North Carolina, Roswell Ham of Mount Holyoke, Franklin Johnson of Colby, Robert Leigh of Bennington, Daniel Marsh of Boston University, Irving Maurer of Beloit, Paul Moody of Middlebury, William Neilson of Smith, George Norlin of Colorado University, Marion E. Park of Bryn Mawr, Walter Scott of Northwestern, and Rufus von Kleinmund of the University of Southern California. I could not read off the names of pro-Republican college professors in the time left to me.

The names alone are obviously insufficient. Let me read from Archibald MacLeish's speech to the American Writers Congress of 1937:

Spain is no political allegory. Spain is not . . . a dramatic spectacle in which the conflict of our time is acted out. These actors are not actors. They truly die. These cities are not stage sets. They burn with fire. . . . How . . . can we refuse our help to those who fight our battles—to those who truly fight our battles *now—now*, not in some future war—*now: now*, in Spain?

When MacLeish finished his appeal for an end to the embargo, Ernest Hemingway rose and delivered the first public speech of his life—and he too spoke on behalf of the Spanish Republic.

Since I cannot tell you of every American who believed in the Loyalists' cause, I'll use Ernest Hemingway as representative of the conscience of a generation. In 1929 he published *A Farewell to Arms.* That novel of World War I was among the most effective of all anti-militaristic books. It contains one of the great passages of our literature. Here is the American reaction to Wilsonian idealism. Here is disenchantment and disillusionment in a paragraph:

I was always embarrassed by the words sacred, glorious, and sacrifice, and the expression, in vain. We had heard them, sometimes standing in the rain almost out of earshot, so that only the shouted words came through, and had read them, on proclamations that were slapped up by billposters over other proclamations now for a long time, and I had seen nothing sacred, and the things that were glorious had no glory and the sacrifices were like the stockyards at Chicago if nothing was done with the meat except to bury it. There were many words that you could not stand to hear and finally only the names of places had dignity. Certain numbers were the same way and certain dates and these with the names of the places were all you could say and have them mean anything. Abstract words such as glory, honor, courage, or hallow were obscene beside the concrete names of villages, the numbers of roads, the names of rivers, the numbers of regiments and the dates.[1]

In 1936, Germans and Italians moved into the Spain he loved, and Ernest Hemingway changed his mind. He decided that some words had meaning after all, that one *can* talk, as the hero of Hemingway's Spanish Civil War novel talks, of Life, Liberty, and the Pursuit of Happiness, of Liberty, Equality, Fraternity, of dead who must not die in vain. Hemingway went to Spain. He wrote short stories and a play about the war; he wrote dispatches published in the *New Republic*

---

[1] Reprinted with the permission of Charles Scribner's Sons from *A Farewell to Arms* by Ernest Hemingway. Copyright, 1929, Charles Scribner's Sons; renewal copyright © 1957, Ernest Hemingway.

and polemics published in *Ken*. He wrote the narrative for Joris Iven's documentary film, *The Spanish Earth*.

The film, like the pastoral scenes in *The Sun Also Rises*, is in part a hymn to the Spanish Earth, to the peasants and to the land. You can see in the film Hemingway's almost mystical attachment to the earth. You can hear it in his elegy for the American dead in Spain:

The dead sleep cold in Spain tonight and they will sleep cold all this winter as the earth sleeps with them. But in the spring the rain will come. . . . This spring the dead will feel the earth beginning to live again. For our dead are a part of the earth of Spain now and the earth of Spain can never die. Each winter it will seem to die and each spring it will come alive again. Our dead will live with it forever. . . . The dead do not need to rise. They are a part of the earth now and the earth can never be conquered. For the earth endureth forever.

Compare these images of the earth to the images in the famous epigraph to *For Whom the Bell Tolls*. "No man is an Iland Intire of it self; every man is a peece of the *Continent*, a part of the *maine;* if a *Clod* be washed away by the *Sea* Europe is the lesse...." Now the Spanish earth and the peasants who worked the earth were attacked by bombers and by tanks, by *Luftwaffe* and *Wehrmacht*. It was not hard for Hemingway and for a host of other Americans to make up their minds. The significance of the Spanish Civil War seemed as clear as the tolling of a bell. And they knew that the bell tolled for them.

I should, of course, be wrong to imply that *all* Americans shared Hemingway's view of Spain or that all Americans spoke out for the Republic. There were a few American Fascists who idolized General Franco as a Blond Beast. *The American Gentile*, for instance, called for American

Fascism, reprinted dispatches from the Nazis' *Völkische Beobachter*, and warned its readers against the "international, Communist-'Protocolic' conspiracy" of our own "Roosevelt-Popular Front, Jew-infested government." The supposedly Jew-infested government refused to see that the Spanish war was the struggle of "Christian Civilization . . . against militant Judaism disguised as Communism." But American Fascists were few.

The only substantial American support for General Franco's *Movimiento Nacional* came from the hierarchy of the American Catholic Church. You have in your readings the statement of 175 Catholic leaders. It is an excellent statement of the hierarchy's position. I have, moreover, read through 223 American magazines for the period 1936–1939 and can report that not one Catholic periodical was for the Republic. Only two Catholic magazines remained neutral on the Spanish war. The first was the *Catholic Worker*—an admirable monthly published by a small group of Catholic anarchists. The other was *Commonweal*—the liberal weekly. *Commonweal* switched, in June of 1938, from a pro-Franco to a neutral position. You have in your readings the editorial that announced this shift and Michael Williams' dissent from the new policy. After taking this stand, *Commonweal* lost 25 percent of its circulation. Catholic journals such as *America* and the *Catholic World* condemned *Commonweal* in the bitterest terms.

The public opinion polls corroborate my reading of American magazines. Pro-Franco sentiment was restricted, for the most part, to Americans of the Catholic faith. Here is the breakdown for the poll of December 16, 1938: Jews, 2 percent for the Nationalists; Methodists, 8 percent; Baptists, 7 percent; Presbyterians,

10 percent; Episcopalians, 11 percent; Roman Catholics, 39 percent.

It is necessary, at this point, to indicate briefly that religious factors were more important, for the *American* response, than economic factors. The economic determinist would argue, if he were a Marxist, that American workers identified their interests with those of the Republic and that American businessmen identified their interests with those of Spanish Fascism. This was not the case. You will recall that, on the polls, the Nationalists received the bulk of their support from the unemployed and from unskilled workers, not from the businessmen. You will recall that Episcopalians were for the Republic while Catholics were often against it. Yet American Episcopalians as a group have a much higher social and economic status than American Catholics as a group. Turn from the polls to the periodical press. While *America*, the *Catholic World, Columbia, Saint Joseph's Lilies*, and a dozen other Catholic journals praised General Franco, the *Commercial and Financial Chronicle, Fortune*, the *Wall Street Journal* condemned him. I scarcely need tell you that American capitalists read the *Wall Street Journal* more closely than they read *Saint Joseph's Lilies*. I was once asked if it were not true that union members were solidly for the Republic. The answer is no. The American Federation of Labor, composed mainly of skilled Protestants, was officially for the Republic; the International Ladies' Garment Workers Union, composed mostly of Jewish workers, was wildly for the Republic; but the C.I.O., composed mainly of Catholic workers, refused to take sides. And it *was* the Catholicism of the workers which made the difference. John L. Lewis told Philip Murray that this was so.

Thus far, I have shown that most Americans were for the Republic and that the embargo of January 8, 1937, injured the Republic. Why did the President pursue and the public support a policy which seemed to run counter to majority will? Basically, for these three reasons: (1) the Catholic opinion which I have already discussed, (2) isolationism, (3) the influence of British policy. I shall take these up in reverse order.

Cordell Hull, our Secretary of State, was determined to follow the lead of Stanley Baldwin and Neville Chamberlain, successively the prime ministers for the Conservative governments of the years of the Spanish war. Long after Anthony Eden refused to condone further "Appeasement," Hull believed ardently in the rightness of British policy. "Britain and France," wrote Hull in his memoirs, "had taken the lead in welding all Europe into a nonintervention committee," and "it would have been unthinkable for the United States to take a contrary course." At almost every juncture in the conduct of American diplomacy, Hull consulted the British Foreign Office. Ambassador Dodd in Berlin warned of Nazi plans, and Ambassador Bowers, in or near Spain, wrote remarkably passionate communications in which he begged—the verb is not too strong—that the Administration change its policy, but the pleas of these two were less persuasive than the dispatches of Ambassador Bullitt in France and Ambassador Kennedy in the United Kingdom. *Their* arguments supported Hull's.

As a factor in the formation of our policy in the middle 1930's, the British lead was probably less important than the predominant mood of isolationism. Although the tradition of aloofness from "European quarrels" is a long one which goes back at least as far as Washington's Farewell Address, isolationist sentiments were at their strongest in the years following the American involvement in World War I. Walter Millis's very influential book *The Road to War* was the historian's complement to Hemingway's *Farewell to Arms,* and both books were filled with a sense of disenchantment with Wilsonian diplomacy. Congressional investigations, chiefly those of the Nye Committee, had discovered that enormous profits had been made in the munitions industry during the war. Many Americans were convinced that they had been hoodwinked into a useless war fought on behalf of a handful of cynical bankers and munitions manufacturers. The disillusionment was so widespread that 73 percent of the voters were, according to one poll, in favor of a national referendum as the necessary condition for declarations of war. The Ludlow Amendment, introduced in 1937, provided for just such a referendum. The Ludlow Amendment was defeated in the House by a scant 21 votes.

When Roosevelt tried, in October of 1937, to stem the tide of isolationism with his famous "quarantine the aggressors" speech, he advocated "positive endeavors to preserve peace." The public response was overwhelmingly antagonistic. At the height of the embargo controversy, on January 9, 1939, the Gallup Poll indicated that only 24 percent of the population favored repeal of the Spanish embargo. Although 58 percent of those listed as "Professional" supported the Loyalists (on poll of December 16, 1938), only 34 percent of this same classification favored repeal of the embargo. On the later poll, only 17 percent of all those approached refused to give an opinion; on the former, 34 percent had refused to respond. So strong, in fact, was the fear of involvement in war, that the embargo against arms to belligerent *nations*

(as opposed to factions) was not repealed until November 4, 1939—over two months after the beginning of World War II.

As important as the mood of isolationism was the political pressure of the hierarchy of the Catholic Church. Franklin Roosevelt feared to raise the embargo because he feared to alienate Catholic voters and thus jeopardize the New Deal. The diaries and memoirs of Roosevelt's cabinet give a fascinating account of the President's dilemma. According to the secret diary of Harold Ickes, "Speaker Bankhead, Majority Leader Rayburn, and Congressmen Ed Taylor had been in to see [Roosevelt, who] said frankly [to me] that to raise the embargo would mean the loss of every Catholic vote next fall and that the Democratic members of Congress were jittery about it and didn't want it done." In his diary, Ickes exploded: "This [is] the cat that was actually in the bag, and it is the mangiest, scabbiest cat ever." Rexford Tugwell, another insider, backs up Ickes' comments: "During the [Spanish] Civil War, the Catholic interest in the United States had influenced policy against the Spanish Republicans; Franklin's compromise then had been hard to explain to liberals, and he had never really tried [to explain it]." The closest student of this particular problem agrees. To the argument that pro-Franco Catholics would have stuck with Roosevelt despite their anger at a (hypothetical) lifting of the embargo, Hugh Jones Parry replies, "The point is less what would have happened than what Democratic strategists feared would happen; and they feared [the] alienation of Catholic votes."

In short, the Spanish embargo remained in effect because most Americans, despite their pro-Loyalist sympathies, shrank from the risk of another war and because Catholic voters important to

Roosevelt's domestic progress were determined to keep the embargo. When, in addition, we consider that any move to succor the Republic would have flouted British policy and left the United States with no allies save Mexico and the Soviet Union, we can see why pro-Loyalist agitation went for nothing, why Roosevelt chose in this situation not to act upon his own convictions.

I think that Roosevelt was wrong not to act. I think that I can show that the pressures for retention of the embargo were less formidable than they seemed. But first, I want to settle a very necessary question. Was the Republic *right*? Were those sympathetic to the Republic more informed than those sympathetic to the Nationalists—or simply more numerous?

Americans who supported the Republic repeatedly said that Spain was a constitutional and democratic Republic. The Republic was said to be legally constituted and, by nature of its democratic character, morally right. But legality is a poor ground on which to build a case for the Republic. The Republic itself was founded by a revolution in April of 1931. Alfonso's claims to the throne were surely more *legitimate*—in the narrow sense— than the Republic's claims to authority. Furthermore, the Communist Party of the United States, the most vociferous organization to shout for legality and constitutionality, was itself pledged to world-wide revolution. American Communists had boasted, with no truth, that Spanish Communists had engineered the unsuccessful revolution of 1934. How could they condemn General Franco for attempting successfully what they themselves had attempted unsuccessfully?

In the second place, the Spanish Republic was not a democratic Republic in our sense of the word "democratic." In the United States, violence is the last resort of a small group of disgruntled citizens. In Spain, however, the *majority* believed in violence. The liberal minority which believed in Anglo-American or in French traditions was swept aside. But democracy must mean something more than majority rule. Democracy, if it is to have any moral force at all, must include the concept of civil rights and of protection of minorities. In Spain, the liberals who *did* believe in civil rights and in protection of minorities were forced from power. President Azaña, a liberal, went into a kind of retirement from public life and despaired of the Republic he had helped to establish. Azaña wrote, "With most Spaniards it is not enough that they themselves can profess and believe what they like. They are offended, they are scandalized, they rise in revolt—if the same liberty is granted to anyone who thinks differently from them." Salvador de Madariaga, the great liberal philosopher and historian, agreed with President Azaña. Madariaga went into voluntary exile and refused to support either side in the Spanish Civil War. Other liberals lost their influence. Some were executed.

Although supporters of General Franco have overemphasized the so-called "Red Terror" in Republican Spain, it is nonetheless a fact that—once the civil war had begun—the Republic was no longer able or willing to guarantee freedom of speech, freedom of the press, freedom of religion, trial by jury. During the Civil War, few Spaniards who dissented from government policy enjoyed the liberties which you and I think of as a necessary part of a democratic society. When groups dissented from the Popular Front, they were ousted from the coalition government. When the groups were small enough, they were suppressed—as was the Trotskyite P.O.U.M.

In short, the Republic was not all its American backers thought it to be. And, as Communist influence increased in Spain, as the Communists wrested power from liberals and socialists, the Republic became constantly less democratic.

And despite all this, I say that the Republic was better than General Franco. Despite all its imperfections, the Spanish Republic was a representative republic. Oppression by majorities is bad; oppression by irresponsible minorities is even worse. Although civil rights were jeopardized under the Republic, civil rights were nonexistent in Nationalist Spain. If small radical parties were suppressed under the Republic—and remember that this is during a civil war—*all* dissent was suppressed under General Franco. The leaders of the Republic often found themselves unable to halt the violence of their followers. The leaders of Nationalist Spain institutionalized violence and made it an ideal. They preached unreason. They shouted, with General Millán Astray, "Down with Intelligence!" The Republic fell short of the democratic ideals proclaimed in its Constitution. The *Movimiento Nacional* achieved the undemocratic ends announced in *its* manifestos.

I have avoided, to this point, the label "Fascist" as a description of Nationalist Spain. But the ideal of Franco's Spain *was* a Fascist ideal. And Fascism explicitly repudiated liberal democracy. Fascism explicitly repudiated the democratic faith in reason and in progress. Let me speak a moment on Spanish Fascism.

The only party allowed in Nationalist Spain was the *Falange Española Tradicionalista y de las Juntas de Ofensiva Nacional-Sindicalista*. The nucleus of this catch-all party (created by General Franco himself) was the *Falange Española y de las J.O.N.S.* This party was itself the merger of two smaller Fascist parties. The first of these was the *J.O. N.S.* This party was anti-Semitic and authoritarian. It opposed liberalism and individualism. It advocated a Catholic state in which all individuals subordinated themselves, free from elections, free from the Jewish mentality, free from the "Mongoloid-imperialistic-Red Stalinists." The other Fascist party was the *Falange Española*. I quote from its founder's most famous speech: "The Fatherland is a transcendent synthesis, an indivisible synthesis, with its own goals to fulfill; and we want this movement . . . to be efficient, authoritarian, an instrument at the service of an indisputable unity, of a permanent unity, of an irrevocable unity, The Fatherland." The first historian of the movement brags that the *Falange* stood for "authority rather than anarchy, militarism and service rather than un-Spanish anti-militarism, and, above all, religious feeling rather than . . . atheism." As leader of the new *Falange,* General Franco proclaimed an end to the "pseudo-wisdom" of liberalism. He promised a Spain of "Bread and Justice" to replace the Republican Spain of Liberty, Equality, Fraternity. The State, wrote General Franco, "will be a totalitarian instrument at the service of national integrity."

At this juncture, I can assemble the pieces of my Spanish puzzle. Franklin Roosevelt requested the embargo of January 8, 1937, because of pressure from the British, from isolationists, from Catholics. Let us assume that the embargo of January 8, and the Neutrality Act of 1937, were both reasonable instruments of foreign policy. They were tried. They failed in the sense that Roosevelt himself admitted, after the war was over, that the embargo policy had been a mistake, that we had unnecessarily injured the Loyalist cause. Is it fair then to castigate the president for a policy that was, although misguided, forced upon him? I think it is, for the president is the *leader* of the nation. He has a responsibility to lead, to educate, to persuade, and, finally, to act as he thinks he should act—despite hostile criticism.

Winston Churchill stood apart from his own Conservative Party and condemned Neville Chamberlain's disastrous policy of appeasement. Anthony Eden resigned his post as Foreign Minister because he could not in good conscience continue to serve that disastrous policy. The Labour Opposition agitated for a change in policy if not in government. The Department of State is not legally bound to follow the Foreign Office's lead. If Cordell Hull and Franklin Roosevelt chose to follow the British, it was their choice. Whatever Hull believed, Roosevelt believed the British were wrong. We cannot excuse him by blaming the British.

In the second place, the isolationists' role can be overemphasized or misunderstood. Yes, the isolationists called for the embargo. No, the isolationists did not demand that the embargo be maintained. Senator Nye, the most important of the isolationists, introduced, on May 2, 1938, a resolution to lift the embargo. He saw the consequences of the embargo and decided that it was intervention against the Republic and not neutrality at all. Charles Beard, another leader of isolationist opinion, caustically denounced the embargo as the reverse of neutrality. Edwin Borchard and William P. Lage, two scholarly advocates of neutrality, argued in their book, *Neutrality for the United States*, that the embargo was misguided: "This was thought to be neutrality legislation. In fact, it was the precise opposite." The embargo was a form of intervention against the recognized government of Spain. In short, the leaders of American isolationism changed their minds on the embargo. Had Roosevelt joined their attempt to sway public opinion, had he used his office to urge repeal on Congress, had he dared—as Henry Stimson suggested—to lift the embargo as part of executive discretion, the leaders of isolationism would have rallied to his side. He ignored the opportunity. Nye's bill never left committee.

I think the president ignored the opportunity because of his fears for the Catholic vote. I have already read you Ickes' and Tugwell's comments on this exertion of Catholic pressure. Although the American hierarchy could not have forced the *adoption* of the embargo, they were able to prevent its repeal.

The final irony is that the Catholic vote was never as monolithic as Franklin Roosevelt and Jim Farley thought it was. Roosevelt did not, in deciding against repeal of the embargo, give in to a minority group. He gave in to a minority segment of a minority group, to the pro-Franco segment of American Catholicism. When quoting to you the statistics on American religious denominations and the Spanish war, I noted that 39 percent of the American Catholics who responded were for General Franco. But 30 percent of them were for the Republic and 31 percent remained neutral. This 61 percent went also leaderless. George Shuster, editor of *Commonweal*, refused to support Franco and Shaemas O'Sheel, writer, backed the Republic; their prestige was little compared to the prestige of Al Smith, Fulton J. Sheen, Father Coughlin, and the entire American hierarchy. The Cardinals of the American Church supported General Franco, and Franklin Roosevelt wrongly assumed they spoke for all American Catholics. He decided to do nothing, but, this, too, was a decision. And more than a decision. It was a contribution to the causes of the Second World War.

What would have happened if Roosevelt had shown a little more courage, if he had supported the best causes abroad as well as at home? What would have happened if he had raised the embargo and even sent American aid to Spain? No one can know for certain, but I think it likely that aid to the Republic would have meant a lessening of Soviet influence in Spain. After all, the leaders of the Republic did not *want* to turn to the Soviet Union for help. They did not want to be forced from power and threatened with imprisonment or execution. They had gone to Moscow because London and Paris and Washington refused their requests. Had the embargo been raised, liberals and socialists like Manuel Azaña and Francisco Largo Caballero would not have been forced to depend entirely on Mexico and the Soviet Union.

It is, moreover, possible that American aid as late as the summer of 1938 might have turned the tide in Spain, might have been enough to allow the Republic to survive. It would have been a Leftist Republic, perhaps as radical as the Labour Government that ruled Great Britain after 1945. It would not have sent Spanish troops to fight on behalf of Hitler's *Wehrmacht* in the Second World War. Franco did.

More importantly, World War II might well have been avoided. The democracies of Western Europe might have saved Czechoslovakia from the sell-out of Munich. They might have convinced Hitler and Mussolini that bourgeois so-

ciety was *not* enervated and enfeebled beyond the point of resistance. The place to stop Hitler and Mussolini was Spain and the time was 1936. And, had World War II been prevented, I need hardly add that the Cold War would not be what it is today. But speculations of this sort become increasingly risky. Let me say the very minimum: it would have been better to have fought Fascism in Spain in 1936 than in the Hawaiian Islands in 1941.

The Spanish Civil War has come to symbolize something to all Americans who lived through the 1930's—and to all Americans who have since come of age. For some it symbolizes the successful struggle of Catholic Christianity against the satanic power of Communist imperialism. For others, of whom I am one, it represents the last great lost cause. I do not want to close sentimentally. But I do think I have provided enough factual and even statistical information to warrant a different kind of argument. Albert Camus came closer than anyone has in summarizing in a paragraph the meaning of the Spanish war. He wrote this in 1946:

It is now nine years that men of my generation have had Spain within their hearts. Nine years that they have carried it with them like an evil wound. It was in Spain that men learned that one can be right and yet be beaten, that force can vanquish spirit, that there are times when courage is not its own recompense. It is this, doubtless, which explains why so many men, the world over, feel the Spanish drama as a personal tragedy.

For my own part, I say that the Spanish tragedy was an American catastrophe. December 7, 1941, was, in the phrase of Franklin Delano Roosevelt, a day of infamy. January 8, 1937, was another.

John G. Gagliardo: A DEFENSE OF AMERICAN POLICY

ON January 8, 1937, the Congress of the United States passed into law that joint resolution which is often called the Spanish Embargo Act. This resolution prohibited the shipment of a wide range of war materials to Spain or to any other country for transshipment to Spain for the use of either party involved in the civil war then raging in Spain.

It is my intention here to argue that the United States behaved wisely in the matter of the Spanish Civil War, with respect not only to the wishes of the vast majority of the American people at the time, but also to the condition of international relations then obtaining and, finally, to the actual issues chiefly involved in the Civil War itself. It cannot, I think, be argued that our government acted always in full awareness of the probable effects of its actions, but simply that these effects were, at worst, no worse than the effects of the alternative actions which our government could have taken, and at best a great deal better.

Let me first of all direct some attention to the question of the extent to which the embargo and a number of associated measures—such as the discouragement of the participation of American citizens in the Spanish Civil War—were representative of the will of the American people. The isolationistic atmosphere in which American neutrality legislation was passed is too well-known to require much comment. I would like to recall, however, that the Senate passed the embargo without a dissenting vote, and that the House of Representatives passed it with only one dissenting vote,

406–1, and to suggest that this is not the sort of vote which can occur in this country in the teeth of major popular opposition. It is indisputable that as the Civil War went on, the virtual unanimity of this initial vote was attenuated: but it is by no means certain that at any point during the war a resolution to lift the embargo would have passed either house of Congress. It would have constituted a violation of the popular will had it done so. Those articulate Americans, numbering undoubtedly in the tens or even hundreds of thousands, who favored the lifting of the embargo, and who gave expression to their views in letters and telegrams to the President and to Congress, in editorials, magazine articles, manifestos, mass meetings, and in many other ways, did not, however ardent they may have been in championing their cause, *did not*, I repeat, represent the views of a majority of the American people.

This question requires some clarification. The proposition has already been put to you by Mr. Guttmann that: "If most Americans *wanted* General Franco to win, the embargo was a useful instrument for attaining the will of the majority. If, on the other hand, most Americans wanted the Republic to survive, then the embargo acted to thwart the will of the majority." Public opinion polls were then cited to you as evidence of the fact that most Americans, indeed at one point by a ratio of more than 3:1, favored the survival of the Republic. This being the case, the embargo thus, *ipso facto*, "acted to thwart the will of the majority."

I will not dispute the public opinion polls; I am quite prepared to admit that they accurately reflected the state of American public opinion. But it requires only a minimum of logic to perceive that there are *two* questions involved here. One is that of the popular sympathy with regard to the opposing camps in Spain; and the other is that of the popular will with regard to American participation or intervention in the war. These are *emphatically* different things! One cannot demonstrate that the embargo acted to thwart majority will by showing that most Americans were sympathetic to the Republic, for the embargo was passed in order to serve, not the vague sympathetic feelings, but the definite will of the American people—to serve a function which the majority of the American people *did* approve: this function was that of keeping the United States free of entangling and perilous international commitments.

This was the function of the embargo as President Roosevelt saw it; he had no doubts that the embargo served the will of the American people, and he made clear his own belief that anything short of an impartial and complete embargo would not effectively serve the desired end. The following statement by Roosevelt, delivered shortly after the passage of the embargo, should illustrate this: ". . . it [is] clear that the civil conflict in Spain involves so many non-Spanish elements and has such wide international implications that a policy of attempting to discriminate between the parties would be dangerous in the extreme. Not only would we, by permitting unchecked the flow of arms to one party in the conflict, be involving ourselves directly in that European strife from which our people desire so deeply to remain aloof, but we would be deliberately encourag-

ing those nations which would be glad of this pretext to continue their assistance to one side or the other in Spain and aggravating those disagreements among the European nations which are a constant menace to the peace of the world."

So much for the will of the people and the enactment of the embargo. What about its maintenance in force from 1937 to 1939? Again, Mr. Guttmann has suggested that Roosevelt did not lift the embargo chiefly because he was afraid of alienating the American Catholic vote. Of those Americans who expressed themselves publicly in favor of Franco, it is unquestionably true that an uncommonly large number were Catholic; it is also true that a large proportion of those who vociferously defended the embargo when it came under attack were Catholic. And I would not argue that Roosevelt, of *all* people, was unaware of the value of Catholic votes to his party and to his own presidency, but I would argue that he had much more important and compelling reasons for retaining the embargo than a fear of alienating Catholic votes. Here, one of those reasons should concern us: and that was that, as all evidence indicates, a substantial majority of the American people during the entire Spanish conflict were distinctly in favor of the purpose which the embargo was to serve. As one recent author has said: "The feeling for one side or the other in the Spanish conflict was purely ideological . . . and does not suggest that Americans wanted the U.S. to intervene actively in Spain. On the contrary, most people were probably in full accord with the statement of the *Commercial and Financial Chronicle* which declared, 'Grievous and fateful as the Civil War in Spain undoubtedly is, it is not an American concern. . . . The experience of 1914–16 should be a warning against allowing propaganda to deflect either the administration or the country at large from a strictly neutral course.' "[1]

In sum, Roosevelt's refusal to lift the embargo was not, as far as domestic politics were concerned, the result of undue pressure exercised by a small portion of the American people, i.e., the Catholics, but the result of Roosevelt's clear understanding of the thorough neutralism of the majority of the American people. The embargo served their will as they themselves saw it, and for Roosevelt to have lifted the embargo would have constituted a betrayal of the mandate of the people with respect to neutrality.

What I have said above notwithstanding, however, I would strongly urge consideration of the possibility that the embargo served a positive goal in the realm of international affairs and diplomacy, as well as the essentially negative or "hands-off" goal implicit in the American popular concept of absolute neutrality. I would suggest, that is, that the embargo was America's contribution to the attempt of the western European nations to establish a workable system of international cooperation as a foundation of collective security. This system, insofar as it had time to be established at all, did not succeed, of course, in preventing the general war it hoped to prevent; but it *might* have done so, given time, and it was in the hope that it would do so that the system was given an admirable try by the western nations until 1939. Let me sketch some background on the system as it related to the Spanish Civil War.

As is well known, the refusal of the United States to have anything to do with the League of Nations and the progressively isolationistic attitudes of a large majority of the American people, together with the uncertain character of French inter-war politics, tended to confer upon England a rather dubious leadership of the democratic western nations. It was not a leadership which the English were very anxious to take, in many ways, for they were nearly as concerned to avoid the complications which could arise from strong-handed international policies as were Americans or Frenchmen; and English domestic problems were just as pressing as the same problems elsewhere. Nonetheless, by default, in a sense, it was England to whom other western nations looked for leadership in facing many of the potentially explosive issues of world politics in the 1930's.

Shortly after the outbreak of the Civil War in Spain, in full cognizance of the international interests which were later to become a conspicuous part of the Civil War, Prime Minister Stanley Baldwin of England was able to convince the French government of Léon Blum that the Spanish situation represented a real threat to international peace, and that the only means of avoiding the danger of general war lay in an agreement, to be entered into by all major powers, which would establish the neutrality and strict nonintervention in the Civil War of all signatories. After the informal discussions on this matter between France and England, it was agreed that France would take the initiative in proposing such an agreement. The text of the proposed agreement was forthcoming on August 15, 1936; by August 24, the chief nations concerned had agreed to the sense of the French proposal, and in September an International Nonintervention Committee consisting of 27 nations was formed. Among these were France, England, Germany, Italy, Portugal, and the Soviet

---

[1] From F. Jay Taylor, *The United States and the Spanish Civil War* (New York, 1956), pp. 137–138.

Union. By the end of 1936, the Committee had agreed upon a system of international control which, if pursued, would have prohibited the shipment of men and arms to Spain for the use of either contending party.

The United States was never formally invited to join this committee. But in full knowledge of the preliminary talks taking place between France and England in August of 1936, the State Department announced officially that the United States Government was following and intended in future to follow "a policy of noninterference in the internal affairs of foreign countries." This was August 11, only four days before the formal French note was circulated to the European powers. The formation of the Nonintervention Committee unquestionably exercised a strong influence upon the formulation of American policy. The American embargo came very close on the heels of the European Committee's decision on a method of control of arms shipments, and our government in January of 1937 publicly warned U.S. citizens that it was a federal penal offense to enlist or to accept, within the jurisdiction of the United States, a commission to serve in the armed forces of a foreign state, and that taking an oath of allegiance to any foreign state amounted to expatriation. It was emphasized that taking service in Spain was "unpatriotically inconsistent" with the policy of nonintervention, and would leave any persons so acting without normal diplomatic protection. These statements were made in January, 1937; they corresponded to the European Committee's agreements on the question of volunteers from the member countries to either side in Spain.

Thus the United States had a very strong reason to pass and to maintain the embargo against Spain—a reason not involved with domestic politics and vote-getting, but rather with the program of international cooperation for collective security planned and led by England. The United States government was fully aware of the extent to which its own neutrality legislation, as expressed in the embargo and administrative orders in the State Department, supported the action of the Nonintervention Committee in Europe. This may be demonstrated by statements of Secretary of State Cordell Hull, who referred on numerous occasions to the European Nonintervention Committee in explaining the position taken by our government on the Civil War. President Roosevelt was similarly disposed towards this issue. He stated that the leading powers of Europe had decided strongly against intervention and that the democracies, at least, were determined to maintain that policy. Both European democracies and the League of Nations, said Roosevelt, "urged very strongly upon us the importance of our arms embargo in the interests of world peace, pointing out the likelihood of a general conflict in Europe unless the Spanish Civil War were kept strictly within the boundaries of Spain."

The American embargo may not be seen outside of the framework of the program of international cooperation suggested by these statements. Certainly there was an awareness on the part of our government, as on the part of the French and English governments, that Germany and Italy represented an unsettling element in international affairs. It was certainly realized that some sort of common action was necessary to prevent the possibility of the increase of world tensions to the point of war. The League of Nations was a dead letter, and the old framework of international diplomacy between nations was seen as the obvious and necessary framework for the realization of common action. By our embargo act, our government attempted to align itself with those nations which were seeking to safeguard the international order. We could not do this by direct alliance; it would have been difficult for us to do it in even such an innocuous way as formal membership in the Nonintervention Committee. American isolationist opinion would not have permitted it. Operating under the difficulties imposed upon it by American public opinion, our government supported the efforts of France and England to prevent Spain from becoming the powder-keg of another world war. This our government did in the only way open to it: by separate and parallel rather than by collective action.

For the United States to have departed from the sort of collective action which France and England had undertaken; for the United States to have struck off on its own and supplied one or the other side in Spain with arms and munitions, would not only have disrupted the unity of the western and Atlantic alliance which later was to be so important, but might very well also have provoked violent reaction within those nations which already had vested interests in the Civil War, and have called down a general war involving the western democracies which had, in effect, neither will nor means with which to fight.

The United States, therefore, contributed in an important way to solidify the concept of collective action in those significant few years immediately preceding the Second World War; the embargo was an important step in the direction of U.S. cooperation with the European democracies—cooperation which later, when the war broke out, was to

mean the ultimate triumph of these democracies over the Axis powers.

One could, of course, object to all this on the grounds that, after all, a general war *did* break out in 1939 in any case, that this system of international cooperation was therefore obviously bankrupt, and that the western powers, and the United States in particular, should have intervened in some direct fashion in the Civil War. With the aid of historical hindsight, for example, many pro-Loyalists in recent years have taxed President Roosevelt with knowing that the U.S. was eventually going to be involved in a struggle with Germany and Italy, and with refusing to join the struggle against the two powers in Spain, at a time when the expansion of Axis influence might have been checked, thus preventing a general war. Roosevelt's refusal to become involved in Spain, in view of his supposed foreknowledge of a future struggle between the U.S. and the Axis, thus becomes either 1) incomprehensible, or 2) a result of a reprehensible timidity in the face of domestic Catholic and isolationist press criticism.

As against this view, I maintain that the evidence supports the conclusion that Roosevelt, like other western statesmen, saw a threat to peace, and that he located it in Germany and Italy; further, that he advocated collective security, of a sort presumably already foreseen in the type of international cooperation represented by the embargo, in order to prevent a war which he still felt was avoidable. He regarded the embargo as a positive measure, within the range of the possibilities of American foreign policy at the time, towards the goal of the preservation of peace. This view, I think, is more consistent than the alternative, and explains Roosevelt's behavior more completely and logically.

If one does assume that the Second World War could have been avoided, it nonetheless remains a fact that it was not, and that the system devised by the western powers to prevent it was not effective. One must, however, take account of the important fact that the threat to world peace which came from Germany and Italy was of a greatly different sort than that which had ever faced statesmen before. The ideological issues involved between democracy and Fascism did not allow of the same methods of compromise which had in previous times been used with success by western statesmen. The German and Italian policymakers were of a different breed than had ever been seen. The policy, indeed the very word "appeasement," which have acquired such ill repute in recent times were regarded, as late as 1939, as a quite legitimate method of attaining to diplomatic compromise. Appeasement was really nothing more nor less than old-fashioned diplomatic bargaining. In any situation of diplomatic tension, elements are always held in reserve by both sides to be used as concessions to the other side for the achievement of as many of one's goals as external circumstances permit. This jealously-guarded storehouse of concessions constitutes an elasticity between differing nations, which alone permits that give-and-take which prevents wars. We have seen the operation of this elasticity in numerous places and on numerous occasions since the end of the Second World War. We could also have seen it operate in the late 1930's. What so baffled western statesmen, and increasingly so, in the situation of the late 1930's was that they seemed always to *give* and never to *receive* concessions —to a point at which they no longer had anything which they regarded as negotiable to give: this was Poland, and

the year was 1939. The elasticity had disappeared. Never before had western statesmen confronted individuals whose assumptions about politics and diplomacy were in so many fundamentals different from their own. It required the rueful lesson of the Second World War to prove the existence and character of such assumptions, and to show that appeasement was not always synonymous with diplomatic bargaining.

In consequence of the above considerations, I would wish to assert two things: first, that an effective opposition to the Axis powers would have had to begin earlier and continue later than the Spanish Civil War, a thing which presupposes such an *entirely* different orientation in western diplomacy than conditions would have permitted that it becomes difficult even to conceive; and second, that of all possible single places for effective western opposition to the Axis, Spain was the worst. The first of these points I will pass over quickly: I mean here simply that the Axis drive for the domination of Europe could not have been deterred by piecemeal action such as intervention in Spain by one or another European or American nation. The only effective means of pounding sense into the Axis governments would have been that of consistently firm opposition by a group of nations which could, if necessary, make its opposition meaningful by resort to force of arms. This would presuppose an international accord of a sort which the League of Nations *did* not provide, and which a firm alliance system *could* not provide under prevailing circumstances—among which popular apathy would rank very high. Certainly after the invasion of Ethiopia by Mussolini, nine months before the Civil War began, only well-concerted action could have deterred the Axis nations: and this kind of action would take time to build, to formulate and to implement.

My second point requires a bit more explanation. I have said that of all places for intervention by the western powers, including America, to occur, Spain was the worst. It was this for several reasons: first, what evidence we have indicates that Mussolini was rather deeply committed, for a number of reasons, to a victory for General Franco, and that any western counter-measures against Franco might well have resulted in a major war effort by Italy, with the possible effect of dragging Germany into the fray in an active role as well. For the western powers, whose goal would presumably have been that of preventing general war, this would have been sheerest folly. Second, it must be kept in mind that there were, after all, *two* foreign ideologies at work in Spain. There were Fascists, it is true, but there were also Communists, who represented an ideology no less odious to the western powers than that of Fascism. It would immensely have complicated the justification for intervention as presented to the peoples of the western nations by their governments for those governments at that time and in that place to have fought alongside the Bolsheviks, for whatever reasons. Third, the Republican government of Spain for which, in terms of Spanish domestic politics, the western powers would have intervened, was by no means a clearly obvious choice of the Spanish people. As will be brought out below, the various candidates of the so-called Popular Front parties polled fewer votes in the elections of 1936 than did the candidates of the right and center parties which were not represented in the government. For foreign powers such as England, France, or the United States to have interfered in the Spanish situation in such a way as to have squelched the opposition to the Popular Front government would have constituted, quite properly speaking, an illegitimate influence upon Spanish politics from which the Axis powers could have drawn a great deal of ammunition for anti-western propaganda, both in their own countries and abroad. Fourth, in connection with my last point, it would be necessary to indicate that the chief antagonists in the Spanish Civil War were not, after all, Communists and Fascists, but Spaniards whose political ideals cannot be defined in terms of any world ideological conflict, except in the vaguest and most general sense, but rather only in terms of a specifically Spanish political situation. It would have been impossible for the United States or any other western power to have begun here a fight against Fascists or, for that matter, against Communists, without at the same time fighting against immensely greater numbers of true Spaniards, whose frame of reference, whose ideals, were purely Spanish and had nothing to do with the great international struggle between the democracies and the Fascist powers.

And yet, of course, there are those who would maintain that here, *here* where the issue of democracy was least clear-cut, was weaker than in almost any other crisis from 1935 until the outbreak of the war in 1939, was most obscured, and legitimately so, by larger issues, by *Spanish* issues—there are those, I repeat, who would maintain that this was the best place for western opposition to Fascism.

It is the fact of the Second World War, of course, which has given rise to that deplorable subjectivity which sees in the Spanish Civil War chiefly but a prelude to the great world war which followed on its heels, rather than chiefly as a domestic conflict with its own issues and logic; a deplorable subjectivity which makes General Franco into a Fascist, and the Spanish Civil War into an international Fascist conspiracy against the freedom-loving people of Spain. I would like to turn now, for the remainder of this exposition, to the Spanish Civil War as a domestic conflict—as a *civil war.* In so doing, I am but following in the footsteps of a number of authors in recent years, who have turned their eyes to the domestic issues involved in the war, and who have correctly reminded us that from the Spanish standpoint, at least, this war never possessed that heavily international character with which partisan writers on both sides outside of Spain have sought to invest it for their own purposes.

My argument here will tend towards the conclusion that any intervention by the United States or any other western powers in the Civil War on the side of the Republic would not have benefited the Spanish people, for it would have perpetuated a government which had proved its inability to cope with the most basic problems of political administration, and which showed absolutely no prospect of amelioration; and that General Franco's government thus presented the better of two alternatives for Spain. In developing my argument, it will be necessary for me first to devote some time to that miserable series of governments in Spain known collectively as "The Republic."

The Republic was instituted in 1931 with a leftist government, and initially enjoyed tremendous popular support. Disillusionment with the directionless governments of Primo de Rivera and King Alfonso XIII made large elements of the Spanish people, in almost all classes, eager for a government which could meet the very real problems which had been ignored for many years. The new Republican government, however, quickly proved itself unable to meet these problems on a truly national scale. The prevalence of localism, particularly among the anarchists, drove the government to propose and to attempt to implement by legislation programs of provincial autonomy for certain regions of Spain. Already, in a sense, by these measures the new government was admitting defeat in any attempt to bring a program of nationally integrated reform to bear upon the problems of Spain. Even more serious than the government's admission of defeat in the localist-regionalist problem was the violent internal dissension within the large parties which chiefly made up this 1931 government. The left Republicans and the Socialists could not agree on a solution to the agrarian situation: the Republicans wanted essentially a nation of individual peasant freeholds, whereas the latter were not to be satisfied with anything less than agricultural collectivization. Another party, the Anarchists, was happy with neither Republicans nor Socialists, whom they saw as both authoritarian and centralist. The suspicion and distrust which existed between these parties to the government would have made rational compromise on the basis of discussion difficult under any circumstances; how much worse, then, that no party in Spain considered it at all improper to impress its program upon the other parties by violence: riots, arson, assassination, bomb-throwing—all of these were considered part and parcel of the normal political process in Spain during the Republic. One of the chief flies in the ointment for the leftists was undoubtedly the Anarchist group. Without any real program, its weight was always thrown into opposition to whatever positive measures might be proposed by other parties; and it could often make its opposition stick, because its labor organization, the so-called CNT, was the largest single organization of its kind in Spain, outnumbering the next largest, the UGT of the Socialists, by some hundreds of thousands of members. It is true that the Socialists and the Anarchists tended to draw closer together, as parties, in the early 1930's: but this was not a rapprochement on the basis of agreement on a positive reform program, but rather on the fundamentally negative tendency of the Socialists to shift towards a violent and revolutionary approach to the solution of Spain's ills—an approach at which the Anarchists had long been adept.

The paralysis of the 1931 government led to widespread disaffection among Spaniards, and in new elections, held in 1933, a moderate rightist government came to power. Not only had there been a shift from the left to the right and center, but the Anarchists, whose uprisings had been suppressed with brutal force by the left Republicans, refused in large numbers to go to the polls at all, more confirmed than ever in their opinion that they wanted nothing to do with the state.

The new government, while no less beset by internal quarrels, was still more harassed than its leftist predecessor by regionalist and other revolts. The opposition leftist parties, feeling absolved from governmental responsibilities now that their own men were no longer in the administration, began a calculated program of destruction of popular confidence in the government. Beginning in December, 1933, with the Anarchists in Aragon, revolts spread to Catalonia, the Basque provinces, and finally to Madrid

and the country at large. The rightist government, hesitant in any case to proceed towards rapid reform, was rendered incapable of doing so because of the continuous necessity for attention to the restoration of basic peace and order. The revolt in Asturias in October of 1934 was particularly hard to suppress, due largely to a working alliance between members of the Socialist UGT and the Anarchist CNT: and it was from the relative success of this union that the left derived the idea of the Popular Front.

When, therefore, new elections were called, in February, 1936, the parties of the left temporarily coalesced into a Popular Front, and won a majority in the Cortes, the representative assembly, of 258 deputies to 215 for the center and right parties. By running a common list of candidates taken from the various parties which made up the Popular Front, the left kept its votes unified, whereas the right and center ran candidates against one another, and thus splintered their vote. For this reason, the Popular Front, while winning the election, actually fell short of the opposition parties' popular vote by 700,000 votes— roughly 8% of the total vote. With the installation of the new government, turmoil and unrest in cities and in rural areas increased still more from their previously high level. The Cortes was paralyzed, becoming little more than a sounding-board for the most violent and vitriolic propaganda. Property losses from rioting were very high, numbers of people were killed, bomb-throwing increased, armed mobs took to the streets, party militias were formed and went into action against one another with increasing violence, and in some cases strikes brought public and private economic life almost to a standstill.

In these few months, from February

to July of 1936, when the Civil War actually began, the complete bankruptcy of the Republic became painfully clear. The rapid decline of popular confidence in the Republic was clearly illustrated by the equally rapid polarization of Spanish politics from the center to the extremes of left and right. In this polarization, the most alarming development was the steady growth of the Communist Party of Spain. In 1931, the Communist Party could count probably no more than 1,000 members; but under the successive disappointments of the regimes of 1931 and 1933, together with the final loss of confidence in the Popular Front government of 1936, the Communists were able to claim as many as 117,000 members by July of 1936. This number was likely an exaggerated one, inflated somewhat by the Communists for their own purposes; but the fact of a considerable growth in party membership cannot be disputed. Still more serious and significant was the Communists' growing influence over the Socialist Party. It will be recalled that the Socialists' only serious competitor for control of the workers' trade-union organizations was the Anarchist group, whose labor organization, the CNT, was larger than that of the Socialists. Since the Communists did not threaten the Socialists' control of worker organizations, the Socialists were not averse to accepting Communist aid in their rivalry with the Anarchists. The misbegotten union of Socialism and Communism in the fateful months preceding the Civil War was facilitated not only by the Socialists' increasing acceptance of violent revolution as remedy for Spain's ills, but also by a considerable sympathy for the Russian revolution by many Spanish workers—a sympathy attested by the circulation of Soviet books and motion pictures. The first issue of this hideous union was the so-called JSU,

a youth organization which put about 100,000 Socialist youth together with about 50,000 Communists. It was the Communists, in a bid for widespread leftist support, who first introduced the epithet "Fascist" to describe the Spanish right wing; it was under the influence of the Communists that such long-time and respected Socialist leaders as Francisco Largo Caballero, Juan Negrin, Alvarez del Vayo, and Fernando de los Rios made public statements of pro-Communist sentiment. As Largo Caballero, for example, said early in 1936: "I am a Marxian Socialist, and Communism is the natural evolution of socialism, its last and definitive stage."[2]

Let me make two important points right here. First, to those who would minimize the Communist threat to Spain in these years by pointing to the relatively small number of party members in 1936, let me say that the real danger lay not so much in the number of party members as in the influence they wielded in larger parties, of which the Socialist is the prime example. Secondly, to those who would maintain that it was only the extraordinary circumstances of the war itself which drove the other parties to accept the aid of the Communists, I would point out that the gruesome embrace of Socialists and Communists took place well before the war began, for reasons not related to the war itself. The rise of the Spanish Communist Party in both numbers and influence antedated the Civil War.

On July 18, 1936, the liberation of Spain from the tyranny of faction, from a 20th-century Hobbesian state of nature, began. Party democracy in Spain was not murdered: it had committed suicide. In a sense, it should have been no sur-

---

[2] Reprinted from *The United States and Spain* by Carlton J. H. Hayes, Copyright 1951, Sheed & Ward, Inc., New York, p. 98.

prise to anyone that a strong hand was taken at this time to save Spain from her own excesses. By July of 1936, even some of the most convinced liberals despaired utterly of the success of the Republic. One of the most famous of them, Salvador de Madariaga, quit the country at this time and refused to give his support to the Republic in which he had once so fervently believed. And in May of 1936, even such a confirmed Socialist as Indalecio Prieto said of his country and of his Republic: "'We Spaniards have never seen so tragic a panorama or so great a collapse as in Spain at this moment. Abroad, Spain is a country classified as insolvent. This is not the road to Socialism or Communism but to desperate anarchism without even the advantage of liberty.'"[3]

Prieto put his finger here directly on the truth: the vaunted liberty of the Republic was not, in fact, liberty, but *license;* it was not freedom, but submission to violent self-destruction. General Franco and a number of fellow officers had observed the gradual decay of Spanish public life under the Republic for five years; they had witnessed the shocking paralysis of the public functions of government and the attendant political fragmentation which manifested itself in the most horrible excesses of violence by parties of every description. They had seen the growth of Communism under the favorable conditions of anarchy. And in the months immediately prior to the war they had seen one of the last effective institutional bastions of Spanish unity, the army, purged by the Popular Front government in what must surely have seemed to them an attempt to break down the determination of the army to stay clear of control by political factions. Finally, on July 13, 1936, occurred the deliberate murder of the leading royalist deputy to the Cortes, Calvo Sotelo; this was the final excess, and the Civil War was on.

There was little ideological uniformity among the generals who led the revolt. Indeed, as Prof. Carlton Hayes has said, the military revolt was remarkably devoid of any particular ideology. All the generals involved had accepted and served the Republic; if some of them were royalists, there were others who were liberal republicans. These were patriotic Spaniards, whose only program was that of putting an end to the chaos which the Republic had brought to Spain. It is undoubtedly true that American public opinion on the Civil War and the Franco government at that time and since has been influenced to a very large extent by the fact that the Spanish liberation was planned by a military group. On this point, I would like again to cite Prof. Hayes: "In the United States and England, army chiefs have been so habitually subservient and so unquestionably loyal to civil government that the average citizen is not likely to understand or feel any sympathy for military revolts abroad; . . . Here is a notable difference between English-speaking and Spanish- or Portuguese-speaking peoples. With the latter, . . . it has long been the army, more than civil government, which has exercised predominance and been the guarantor of order and security against anarchy and subversion."[4] He goes on to point out that there was nothing new or shocking about the Spanish military revolt of 1936; that there were many precedents for it in Spain and the rest of the Spanish and Portuguese world; and that such precedents had by no means universally presented the picture of reactionary dictatorships, but also

---

[3] Quoted in Hayes, *op. cit.,* p. 100.

[4] Quoted in Hayes, *op. cit.,* p. 102.

that of liberal constitutionalism.

This is perhaps not the place for a disquisition on American *naïveté* with regard to the role of the military establishment in history; I would, however, recall that in recent years we have seen the army, notably in Korea and Turkey, dispossess dictatorial and undemocratic regimes in order to bring governments in greater measure into harmony with popular needs. It is devoutly to be hoped that the insights we have gained from experiences such as these will make us a little less predisposed to see in every military man a minion of the devil, and to realize, in more specific terms, that General Franco and his military group were not simply a bloodthirsty band of vicious adventurers bent on the rape of Spain.

Nor was General Franco a Fascist. It is, I hope, not superfluous to point out the necessity of distinguishing political complexions to the extent of not labelling every liberal-minded reformer a Communist, nor every nationalist a Fascist. And a nationalist is precisely what General Franco was. Even the most superficial research into Franco's background would reveal the striking dissimilarities between his personality and attitudes and those of Hitler and Mussolini, for example. His acceptance of military aid from Germany and Italy did not imply acceptance of their ideas, which he himself said were absurd for Spain. Hitler and Mussolini used the Civil War for their own purposes—and these were not the same as those of General Franco. A wall of real suspicion always existed between the Franco government and the Axis powers. Franco, let it be recalled, managed, by some delicate and creditable maneuvering, at the height of Axis power, to keep Spain neutral. And the famous "Blue Division," which he sent to the Russian front, was sent, first, as a sop

to Hitler, in order not to incur Axis enmity at a time when the latter occupied virtually all of western Europe, and secondly, to fight Bolsheviks, whom Franco had good reason to hate.

Franco's ideals were not Fascistic: if one keeps the specifically Spanish situation fully in view, Franco's statements on totalitarianism and authoritarianism have a much different significance than the same words in the mouths of Mussolini and Hitler. The Spanish state would be totalitarian in the sense that it would not, in future, be a factious state of this or that conniving party or group of parties, but rather a national Spanish state to which all Spaniards would be able to look with confidence; and it would be authoritarian in the sense of the object for which the war was fought—it would be sufficiently authoritarian to insure that the history of the Republic from 1931 to 1936, a history of violence, terror, and unrestrained party strife, would not be repeated. The Falangist Party of which Franco became the head was not the same Falangist Party, except in name, which had earlier espoused properly Fascistic ideals, for after the Civil War began it came to include large elements of earlier rightist and even centrist parties, so that it became, so to speak, a kind of Popular Front of the right. Franco's government since his victory in the war has been very little reminiscent of the Fascist governments which existed elsewhere in Europe; and political repression, while occasionally harsh, has served not so much to deprive all Spaniards of all of their liberties as to confirm the vast majority in the enjoyment of most of their liberties. It is difficult to know just what percentage of the Spanish people supported each side in the war. Strangely enough, in the various regions of Spain there was a tendency for claims of popular support to reach 100%

for that side whose armies happened to occupy the district at the time. But one thing appears increasingly clear: the various elements of the Republican armies, with the exception of the international brigades, fought less for the Republic than for their own parties. Once the Communists became strong in the wartime government, they organized and led, but aided by Socialists and Republicans, a campaign of terrorism and assassination against strongly non-Communist elements of the Loyalists; and, incredible as it may seem, large numbers of men on both Socialist-Republican and Anarchist sides in Valencia were actually held back from the front by their party leaderships because of a fear of renewal of party strife once the war was over.

I do not know, I think, how in this case one is to separate the so-called democratic goals of the Republic from the manner in which they were (or were not) carried out in reality. In 1932, the famous philosopher José Ortega y Gasset said of the authors of the 1931 constitution: "These Republicans are not the Republic."[5] But how long could honest Spaniards believe it possible to separate the *idea* of the Republic from its lamentable implementation in a real world? The most respected intellectual in Spain, the republican Miguel de Unamuno, later in the same year protested the police methods of the leftist government which, he said, were worse than the infamous Inquisition—for even it "was limited by a guarantee of rights."[6] The government of General Franco was not and is not a democratic government; it was not and is not a fundamentally reform-minded government, although it has made some progress along these lines, particularly with regard to the at-

traction of foreign capital to Spain—without which the Spanish economy cannot hope for much amelioration. Nonetheless, I would not maintain that the goals of General Franco are better, or worse, than the goals of the Republic—whatever those were. But I would maintain that the government of General Franco was a better government for Spain than was the government of the Republic; I would maintain that in the eight years of its existence, in peace and in war, the Republic proved itself a thousand times over unworkable, unmanageable, inept, bungling: at best paralytically benevolent, at worst maliciously terroristic; and finally, that no redeeming feature of this Republic stands out, in historical perspective, to afford even the slightest evidence that anything but a continuation of the same exhausting party strife would have followed a victory of the Loyalists in the Civil War.

In conclusion: I have tried in this exposition to make three basic points with regard to America's stand on the question of neutrality legislation relative to Spain. First, that any stand other than that taken by our government would have violated the will of the vast majority of the American people. Second, that the American stand may be seen as a positive contribution to a system of international cooperation designed to prevent a world war, and that intervention in this time and in this place would have been a mistake in itself. And finally, that the Spanish conflict, viewed as the basically domestic affair which it was, took a better course, for Spain, without western intervention than it quite likely would have with it. Spain is a troubled country, with an uncertain future. General Franco and his type of rule may well not be the answer to Spain's many problems; but the Republic *certainly* was not.

[5] Quoted in Hayes, *op. cit.*, pp. 90–91.
[6] Quoted in Hayes, *op. cit.*, p. 93.

Suggestions for Additional Reading

The Age of Roosevelt is admirably set forth in Arthur M. Schlesinger, Jr., *The Age of Roosevelt* (Boston, 1957–1960). The first three volumes of this history bring Roosevelt's administration up to the time of the Spanish Civil War. Biographies of Roosevelt are many. The interested student should begin with James M. Burns, *Roosevelt: The Lion and the Fox* (N.Y., 1956). The best general account of American foreign policy in this period is William L. Langer and Everett S. Gleason, *The Challenge to Isolation* (N.Y., 1952). On arms embargo legislation, the student may consult Robert Divine, *The Illusion of Neutrality* (Chicago, 1962). Students who wish to press further for the details of American policy should consult Claude G. Bowers, *My Mission to Spain* (N.Y., 1954). The Congressional Record and the State Department's publications of the documents of American foreign policy provide much information and some insights into American policy.

The most available book on the Spanish Civil War is Hugh Thomas, *The Spanish Civil War* (N.Y., 1961). Thomas avoids generalization and judgment and provides the most nearly accurate chronicle available at this time. Thomas should be supplemented by Gerald Brenan, *The Spanish Labyrinth*, 2nd ed. (Cambridge, Eng.; 1950). Stanley G. Payne's *Falange* (Stanford, 1961) is an excellent account of Spanish Fascism from its origin to the present. David T. Cattell's monographs,

Communism and the Spanish Civil War (Berkeley, 1955) and *Soviet Diplomacy and the Spanish Civil War* (Berkeley, 1957), are both good. Of the memoirs of those who fought, George Orwell's *Homage to Catalonia* (London, 1938) is the masterpiece.

Two books give a general account of American responses to the Spanish war. F. Jay Taylor's *The United States and the Spanish Civil War* (N.Y., 1956) is a fine study of American diplomacy with some attention given to the domestic sources of foreign policy. Allen Guttmann's *The Wound in the Heart: America and the Spanish Civil War* (N.Y., 1962) attempts to analyze American responses and interpretations, to show *why* Americans reacted as intensely as they did to the Spanish war. Edwin Rolfe's *The Lincoln Battalion* (N.Y., 1939) is a survivor's account of the Americans who fought in Spain. Despite the political commitments of the author to the Soviet Union's policy in Spain, the book is excellent. Of American memoirs, the best are Alvah Bessie's *Men in Battle* (N.Y., 1939), Steve Nelson's *The Volunteers* (N.Y., 1953), and Sandor Voros's *American Commissar* (Philadelphia, 1961). These accounts are all pro-Loyalist; no American fought on the Nationalist side.

The Spanish Civil War brought forth an extraordinary number of novels, plays, stories, and poems. Among the best are these: Ralph Bates, *Sirocco and Other Stories* (N.Y., 1939); José María Gironella, *The Cypresses Believe in God* (N.Y., 1955); Ernest Hemingway, *For Whom the Bell Tolls* (N.Y., 1940); André Malraux, *Man's Hope* (N.Y., 1938); Gustav Regler, *The Great Crusade* (N.Y., 1939); Edwin Rolfe, *First Love and Other Poems* (Los Angeles, 1951); Norman Rosten, *The Fourth Decade and Other Poems* (N.Y., 1942); Boris Todrin, *Seven Men* (N.Y., 1938). Hemingway, Rolfe, Rosten, and Todrin are American.

Periodical literature on the Spanish Civil War is enormous. Students interested in the spectrum of American opinion from political Right to political Left should consult the following journals for articles and editorials on the Spanish war: *The American Review* (Fascist), *The National Republic* (Conservative), *The American Mercury* (Conservative), *America* (Conservative-Catholic), *The Catholic World* (Conservative Catholic), *Commonweal* (Liberal-Catholic), *The Atlantic Monthly* (Liberal), *Christian Century* (Liberal-Protestant), *The New Republic* (Liberal), *The Nation* (Liberal), *The Modern Monthly* (Socialist), *Partisan Review* (Socialist), *New Masses* (Communist), and *The Vanguard* (Anarchist). For an extensive bibliography of American books, pamphlets, articles, novels, plays, stories, poems, films, paintings, sculptures, dances, and musical compositions on the Spanish Civil War, see Guttmann (above). For a bibliography on the Spanish Civil War itself, see Thomas (above).